The Event Groom's Handbook

Jeanne Kane
Lisa Waltman

 THRESHOLD BOOKS

First published 1983 by
Threshold Books Limited,
661 Fulham Road, London SW6 5P2

Second Impression 1985
Third Impression 1986
Revised Edition 1989

Edited by Eileen Thomas and Barbara Cooper
Designed by Alan Hamp
Editorial Assistant Suzannah Staley

British Library Cataloguing in Publication Data

Kane, Jeanne
      The event groom's handbook.——2nd ed.
      1. Eventing horses. Care
      I. Title   II. Waltman, Lisa
      636.1'083

ISBN 0–901366–07–2

Typeset in Great Britain by
Phoenix Photosetting, Chatham
Printed in Great Britain by Mackays of Chatham PLC, Chatham, Kent

Contents

Acknowledgements

Since we are used to working with horses and not with words, the writing of this book has been a new and eye-opening experience, which would not have been possible without the patient help and unflagging support of so many people on both sides of the Atlantic. We would like particularly to express our thanks and appreciation to the following:

The Publisher, Barbara Cooper, who through her enthusiasm for the subject and her confidence in us, took the bold step of commissioning the book, and who has seen it through each stage of writing, editing, design and production; Eileen Thomas, the Executive Director of the United States Combined Training Association, who took our 'raw material' and spent many hours of her limited spare time moulding it into a coherent whole; Jack Le Goff for his encouragement and for writing his generous Foreword; Suzannah Staley for her expert assistance in the overall co-ordination of the project; Alix Coleman, Cappy Jackson, and Sue Maynard, who searched their files for just the right illustrations; Kit Houghton who also went to great trouble to take special photographs of specific subjects; Paul Farrington for his notes on the vital signs; and Linnea Wachtler for her diagram.

Throughout the book you will find the pronouns 'he', and, occasionally, 'she', used for rider and groom respectively. We mean no rôle distinction: both men and women can become top riders or top grooms as long as they have the right temperament, enthusiasm, and qualifications needed to achieve a good job well done. We should also point out that as the book is truly a product of Anglo-American co-operation, the English used in it should be universally understood; however the differences in meaning that occasionally occur are explained in the Glossary.

Finally, we hope that you will find this book useful, and that you will enjoy reading it as much as we enjoyed writing it.

Jeanne Kane
Lisa Waltman

Picture Credits

Adelaide Advertiser: page 72. **Douglas Catto:** page 171. **Alix Coleman:** pages 15, 62, 69, 71, 82, 86, 112, 116, 117, 121, 123, 154. **Findlay Davidson:** page 140. **James Deutschmann:** page 92. **Kit Houghton:** pages 11, 63, 77, 80, 96, 110 (left), 113 (bottom), 114, 120, 146, 156. **Cappy Jackson:** pages 17, 79, 94, 95, 98, 106, 110 (right), 113 (top), 115, 119, 126, 136, 151, 158. **Jeanne Kane:** pages 23 (left), 28, 33, 59 (right), 67, 91, 122, 124, 134, 138, 144. **Barry Kaplan:** page 20. **Sue Maynard:** pages 14, 22, 32, 43, 50, 51, 54, 59 (left), 73, 75, 87, 101, 103, 125, 127, 129–132, 143. **J McClung:** page 153. **Warren Patriquin:** pages 18, 19, 48, 52, 53, 85. **Phelps Photography:** pages 13, 23 (right), 128. **Anne Thomas:** pages 148, 149. **Linnea Wachtler:** page 162. **Moya Waltman:** page 9.

Foreword

Anyone who has been involved with horses for any length of time knows how difficult it is to find and keep good help. But if you are lucky enough to have a top Stable Manager, miraculously all your staff problems seem to vanish and your barn functions almost by itself, with healthy and happy horses.

I first met Jeanne Kane when she came to groom for a rider who was training with the United States Equestrian Team in South Hamilton, Massachusetts. Since my Stable Manager at that time was unable to work, following a bad skiing accident, I found myself searching for a replacement. Because it is commonly believed that experience and qualification only come with age, I observed with suspicion this twenty year-old young lady's work and actions, both with horses and with people, having millions of doubts about her being able to cope with the important and different aspects of the job in question.

However, I realised very rapidly that my worries were unfounded and that despite her young age she was going to be a top Stable Manager. Her total dedication, together with her intelligence, her constant desire to improve her standards, and her enthusiasm and ability to communicate with people were an invaluable help to me as a coach, and allowed me to concentrate on the other facets of my responsibilities, knowing that the job was well done in the stable.

It is a reflection of Jeanne's personality and spirit of team work that she has written this much-needed book, in collaboration with another very qualified person, Lisa Waltman. Thanks to her dual UK/US citizenship, Lisa has been able to work with horses on both sides of the Atlantic, always at the top levels of the sport. Her early experience was gained with former World Champion, Lucinda Green, and she later worked for Olympic Gold Medallist, Mike Plumb. During the 1984 Olympics she and Jeanne Kane helped in the stabling organization at Los Angeles.

The combination of those two horse-loving people, sharing together their experience of all levels of Eventing in the United States, as well as in Europe, has produced a remarkable book. Its contents reflect the great care that top grooms take in all the different aspects of grooming an Event horse and stable managing an Event barn, which to me is certainly one of the most complex and sophisticated jobs in the horse business.

I wrote the original Foreword when *The Event Groom's Handbook* was first published in 1983, and since then there have been two further printings. Now we have this revised edition, which proves that the book is still very popular. I wish it further success, and recommend it to all in the sport of eventing who want to learn about the care of horse and rider.

Jack Le Goff

Introduction

The sport of Eventing has been, and still is, expanding at a tremendous rate – in Britain, the USA, several parts of Europe, Australia, New Zealand, and even Japan. From its origins as a test of endurance and versatility for the cavalry it has grown into an Olympic sport which attracts attention far beyond the bounds of the equestrian world.

In its early days it was purely for amateurs: anyone with a hunter could 'have a bash' and get a great deal of fun and excitement – if not prestige and prizes – from it. Nowadays the standards demanded are far above the capabilities of many of our forefathers. Competition is fierce and though the financial rewards are not particularly high, the national and international renown that one can achieve are well worth the effort.

It is not only standards that have become higher. So have costs, not just of buying horses but of their keep and all the necessary extras. Inevitably this has led to fewer people being able to take up Eventing seriously, though sponsorship is slowly but surely coming to the rescue of many promising and established competitors. Thus pressure is brought to bear even more heavily on riders to do well and give their money's worth.

Gone are the days when a horse was a family pet, living in the garden, being ridden after work and at weekends, and occasionally picking up a rosette or two. Today, though the amateur/professional debate continues, there is no doubt that most top Eventing establishments are, in essence, run professionally, with a well-trained full-time staff and perhaps ten or more valuable horses – from proven world beaters to possible stars of the future.

To take charge and oversee this kind of set-up a very special type of person is called for: who is dedicated as well as knowledgeable; who has the ability to take responsibility and make decisions; who cares intensely for the well-being of the horses; who has a sharp eye for detail; is flexible and sensible enough to act with calm efficiency in any situation; and has a sense of humour strong enough to overcome the disappointments which inevitably beset the world of competition. This paragon must also be prepared to remove some of the burden from the rider's shoulders.

So an Event groom today is more than merely a labourer whose sole duties are mucking out and grooming: the job is inevitably becoming a highly skilled profession in which the aim is to produce and care for physically and mentally fit horses capable of competing successfully at a very high level. Veterinary and horse-management techniques are now so sophisticated that looking after competition horses is fast becoming a science. In fact, 'groom' is now a misnomer that should be changed to 'equine technician'.

As a groom, your reward is not just the glory of your charge winning a prize but also the immense satisfaction of knowing that you have done absolutely everything within your capabilities to turn out horse and rider immaculately, and to help them into the winner's enclosure. A hard-working, dedicated groom is in effect one side of an equilateral triangle, the other two sides being the horse and the rider. Remove one of the sides and the remaining two will collapse. You are part of a closely-knit team – an integral cog in an important wheel. By realising the enormous responsibility of your position and acting with appropriate common sense and diligence, the appreciation and respect you rightly deserve will be yours, and you will prove that you can be as irreplaceable as one of the horses.

It is, however, an exacting job and is definitely not as simple as is sometimes imagined. Not only is it physically tiring, but it is also a mental strain. For instance, such a small, trivial lapse as the overlooking of a tack-check may lead to the breaking of a rein or a stirrup leather and could rob your team of success. The thought, 'If only I had checked it' will live with you forever. We hope that by emphasising the necessity for a methodical and meticulous régime in preparing yourself and your horses for an Event, this book will eradicate such mishaps.

Our aim in writing the book is to help grooms and, we hope, riders, by sharing the ideas, methods and experiences that we have used successfully as international Event grooms working in Britain, the USA and other parts of the world over the past twelve years. Obviously there are many ways of skinning a cat, so some of our methods and suggestions, which have evolved from personal experiences and preferences, are meant only as guidelines and are not obligatory for success in Eventing.

We hope and believe that by reading this book, by implementing or adapting some of our ideas, and by living up to the motto, 'Be Prepared', you, too, will be able to stand back at the end of the day and take great pride and satisfaction in a difficult and demanding job well done.

CHAPTER ONE

The Groom's Rôle

At first glance, a groom's rôle is self-explanatory. A groom is a person who looks after horses, who grooms and exercises them, and who generally makes sure that everything is run efficiently, so that both horse and rider are happy. Often the rider and groom are one and the same person; many people look after their own horses and have help only at the competitions.

Grooming competition horses, however, is a far more specialised and demanding job. It requires someone with an understanding of the sport and of the rider's ultimate goals – and someone with the strength of character to handle the extra pressures and responsibilities.

Most careers with horses involve long hours of work in all weathers, often for little financial reward. So we are talking about a life-style rather than a conventional nine-to-five job. As grooms we work with horses because we love them and because we derive great satisfaction from our involvement with the horse and from knowing that we are an integral part of our rider's success.

So what is it about the world of Eventing that draws us to it? What sort of people are we? To begin with, the fact that an Event horse and rider have to be experts in three different disciplines immediately triples the interest and challenge for the groom. The Event horse is the epitome of an all-round athlete, and the sport today has reached such a high level of competition on a world-wide basis that it is no longer good enough to be just 'all right' in the Dressage and Show Jumping phases, and to hope that a brilliant cross-country round will win the day. To have any chance of success at all, horse and rider must be experts in all three phases.

So as a groom you have to appreciate that the horse you are looking after is three competitors rolled into one, and you must know how best to care for this very special animal. Maybe like us you find Eventing the ultimate challenge. Without doubt there are worthwhile 'perks', such as travelling abroad; and grooming at an Olympic Games has to be the high peak of any groom's career. The work is certainly varied and exciting, and can give incredible satisfaction, because in international Eventing, more than in any other equestrian sport, the groom is just as important as the rider or the horse.

The responsibility can be awesome. As well as the obvious task of taking care of the horses and the daily chores of running a yard – in itself a full-time job – there are also the hidden obstacles to be tackled. Preparing for a Three-Day Event is a long, slow process. It takes about three to four months to transform a shaggy, vacationing horse into a fit and ready-to-run competitor. If you manage to live through all the traumas that those months may unfold, you will stand a fair chance of surviving the actual Three-Day Event without acquiring too many grey hairs.

In show jumping or racing, missing a show or a race because of injury or

The quiet moment before the cross-country in which the groom goes over a mental check list. Is she ready for any eventuality? Note the warm rugs and the safety knot in the end of the reins.

unfitness usually only entails a wait of perhaps a week until the next opportunity arises. But in our sport there is usually only one Three-Day Event at the end of the season that the rider can aim for, and if something happens to prevent him from competing there could well be a long wait for the next chance – maybe as much as six months. Tension can build up, nerves can be stretched to the limit, and it is part of your job as a groom to be able to handle this tension within yourself and at the same time to support and pacify your rider.

Some people work better under pressure and some crumble – and at a Three-Day Event the pressure is certainly on. The rider will be wound up to bursting point, so no groom can afford to be the crumbling type. While you may be worrying about material things, the rider will be having an inward battle with his nerves; and doubts about his own or his horse's abilities will make him more difficult than usual to deal with; on top of which he may have the extra pressure of living up to the expectations of owners and sponsors.

Nerves affect riders in many different ways. They will often become extra picky and can be really irritating – checking and double checking tiny little details and suddenly changing equipment at the last minute. All these things can drive a groom to distraction, but at such moments you will take a deep breath and make a great effort to be tolerant and understanding. Most probably after the Event is over and done with, you will both be able to recall the times when you were at each other's throats, and will have a good laugh about them.

One of the biggest problems to be overcome on the part of the groom is possessiveness. You are often closer to the horse than the rider, for you are the one who has spent the most hours of each day with your charge and should, by this point, know the animal like the back of your hand. Thus you may become resentful, thinking you know best, which can only lead to trouble.

One of the most desirable traits in a groom – and one of the reasons for having the job in the first place – is the ability to get under the skin of the horse that you are caring for and to notice and understand all the tiny idiosyncrasies of each individual animal. You must realise that this is why you have been employed – this is your gift and your contribution towards a successful team. The trap to avoid is the one of thinking that you can do the riding, too. If you are totally honest with yourself you will admit that your skills lie in caring for the horse and you will be proud of the fact that expertise in the stable is just as important as the rider's skill on the horse's back.

On the practical side, a groom's job may be broken into two parts: your life at home and your life at competitions. At home you must keep the horses mentally and physically fit and well, making sure that they are getting the right amount of food, hay, grooming and attention. You must build up a rapport with each individual horse, so you will know each one inside out and will, therefore, instinctively be aware when something is not quite right. You must keep the whole yard running smoothly, ordering bedding and feed, keeping up to date with shoeing and veterinary work and making sure that all the tack is in tip-top condition – attending, in short, to all the normal duties of a groom. But, in addition, you must always be looking forward and planning for the next competition and you must be prepared for the unexpected.

Part of any grooming job involves getting along with other people, especially in a big yard where there may be trainee grooms or students. So here we find yet another angle to the responsibilities of an Event groom – the ability to teach and to set a good example. The people working under you must be well instructed, because once you are on the road and off to the Events, they will often find themselves in sole charge of the horses remaining at home, and they must be capable and confident of doing the job efficiently in your absence. If you have taught them well you should have no qualms about leaving them for a week or two.

Teamwork: an international rider with her grooms and horse, ready to set out for an Event.

In your other rôle as travelling groom you will often find that you are the person doing most of the driving, so a knowledge of motor mechanics, map reading, and tyre changing is essential – as well as at the same time being able to handle the horses in the van.

While at Events, a groom should follow normal 'home' routine as closely as circumstances will allow; this will help the horses to settle in more quickly in strange surroundings. The ability to be flexible, inventive and capable of improvising is one of your most useful assets. You may arrive at an Event to find facilities somewhat lacking, so be prepared for anything – and for a Three-Day Event this means packing every single piece of equipment that you think is necessary, even if the tack room is cleared of everything except the sink. You never know what you may need when you get there – from a pair of wire cutters or twenty feet of hose pipe, to a boot-lace.

So all in all an Event groom today is someone whose make-up is a mixture of horse sense and common sense; someone fired by a love of horses, who is able to work towards distant goals in a methodical and meticulous way; someone who can laugh at the silly things instead of getting worked up about them and, above all, who can realise her worth as part of a team. You must also keep a realistic view of life and be able to handle disappointments along with successes – all in the same vein of good sportsmanship. All being well, you will never lose sight of the main reason for becoming an Event groom in the first place – the fact that it is both fun and challenging. As soon as these two aspects start to wane, it is time either to take a vacation or to re-consider your involvement with the sport and what it actually has to offer you.

But before we make the groom's rôle out to be a twenty-four hour, seven-days-a-week marathon, let us emphasise how important it is to get away and totally relax from this all-enveloping career. No one can work at their best if they are not rested and if they have few or no outside activities.

Often it is unavoidable to live anywhere other than on the job, but if you have the choice you should try to move into your own cottage or apartment so that at least you have a place of your own – somewhere just to get away from it all and unwind. No matter how well you might get along with your employer and co-workers, it can be extremely difficult and a great strain to have to work, eat and sleep in each other's company twenty-four hours a day, especially during the Event season when tempers may be stretched and when days off are a rare occurrence.

A trap that many horsy people fall into, without even realising it, is that of being able to talk about nothing but horses. Beware! There is a world out there that is concerned with other matters. It is easy to fool yourself into believing that the horses cannot survive without your undivided attention. You must see to it that this is not the case, and you must realise that life will be much happier for all concerned if you can manage to get away from the intense atmosphere of the competition yard once in a while, just to let your hair down and have a good time. So find outside hobbies and friends and make time to relax. It is amazing how good it is after a long hard day to take a shower, get dressed up and go out for an evening of fun.

There are always parties to go to at Events – more so in the United States than in England where unfortunately there is still something of a barrier between grooms and riders. However, the need to have fun and relax is often filled by grooms making their own spontaneous fun and organising their own parties. Provided that you keep your priorities in order and your rôle in perspective; that you have done your job to the best of your ability and the horses do not suffer; and that you are always in a fit enough state the next morning to do your work as well as ever, no one is going to criticise you for relaxing for a while.

As long as there is always a challenge and as long as you can reap satisfaction from the daily life at home – realising that trips abroad and to Three-Day Events are not going to happen every week (probably more like once or twice a year); as long as you feel that there is always something to learn and that you are happy, you will be the one who will get the most out of the job and, probably, put the most into it. It is a job that often goes unpraised, that is more often than not tiring and subject to difficult weather conditions, but it is so very vital to the success and good will of what is to us the greatest of all sports.

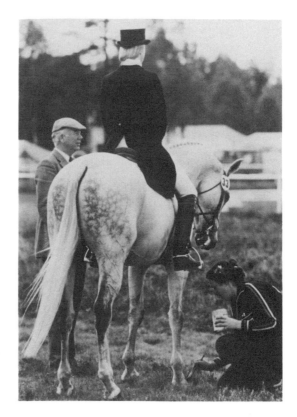

Teamwork: rider, horse, groom and trainer at the beginning of a Three-Day Event. Note the fine example of a pulled tail.

13

CHAPTER TWO

Preparation

In any sport the time spent actually competing is miniscule compared to the number of hours spent in the training and preparation work. In writing a book for grooms it would be pointless to talk solely about the actual competitions. How to reach competition stage and the work involved on the way are equally important. For the Event groom the daily running of the yard and the caring for the horses is the unsung and unglamorous part of the job, but it is vital if you want to do well. Therefore if you realise how important the ground work is at home and how every little detail will affect the final outcome you will be able to work from day to day knowing that everything you do has a purpose and is worth doing well. It is nearly always the little things that can be your downfall, such as unchecked tack that breaks half-way round a cross-country course; a mishap of this kind makes you want to crawl into a tiny hole, because you know that it could have been prevented.

We have no power over natural disasters but we can do a great deal to make sure that nothing is left to chance. For a groom this is achieved by being conscientious, meticulous and methodical. Apply the proverb, 'Look after the pennies and the pounds will look after themselves' to grooming and the chances are that you will arrive at an Event fully prepared, with fit and ready-to-run horses, and you should end up doing really well.

So let us get down to the structure of a well-run eventing yard. The number one priority must always be the horse's well-being. All else must take a back seat.

Keeping a diary

The easiest way to remember something is to write it down, and keeping a

This is what a well-run Event yard should look like. Note the meticulous attention to detail.

diary is essential in the running of an efficient yard. The more horses you have to look after the less chance there is of your being able to remember little details concerning a horse six months later.

At the beginning of each year, buy yourself a large hard-backed diary that will give you enough space to have two or three lines per day for each horse in your charge. You can then write in all the important dates that you need to remember, such as worming, inoculations, teeth-floating, and the dates of Events. Ideally, the diary should have a few blank pages at the back for inventories, both of your own equipment and also for that of any boarders. A section kept exclusively for recording veterinary visits is a great help, and here you should note the date, the horse involved, and the treatment and medication prescribed. This will give you a very useful cross-reference point. For example, once you have found the date when 'Dobbin' had a colic drench you can look up the relevant day in the diary for a more detailed record of the circumstances relating to such treatment.

On a daily basis you should record the work done by each horse, the condition of the legs after the work, whether he was shod that day – and anything out of the ordinary, such as a loss of appetite or treatment with a new medication. By doing this every day you will build up a detailed picture of each horse's well-being and work progress which will serve as a valuable reference for many years to come.

Unless you are doing much of the fitness work yourself, it is not necessary to record the exact details of every piece of fast work done by each horse. It is just important that you record that they did do fast work on a particular day – the minutes and seconds of a half-speed canter are notes that most riders make and keep for their own reference. So, for example, a page from your diary may look like this:

TUESDAY, 24 FEBRUARY

Star: 1 hour hack, trotted up hills. ½-hour dressage schooling. Legs cool and unfilled. Shod p.m. – new shoes with stud holes. [Note: This record will serve as a reference for checking that the blacksmith's bill is correct.]

Sandy: Hacked to the plains and did his first work-out of the season. Over-reached and cut the heel on his near fore; not serious – flap of skin cut off; foot tubbed with Epsom Salts and cleaned with hydrogen peroxide, and an ointment applied under vet wrap. Trotted him out in the afternoon and he was sound. Legs were a little warm, so he was bandaged all round afterwards for comfort and support, and to promote circulation. Increased his oats by two pounds a day, to make up for the harder work he is in now.

Samson: New horse, arrived today. Up-to-date on 'flu and tetanus injections. Trotted up sound – his legs are a little stocked-up but previous owner said this was part of his make-up. Turned him out for ¾ hour in the paddock and hacked out for one hour. Gave him a bran mash with two pounds of oats, p.m. Starting tomorrow will slowly build this up to regular rations.

Legs, their care and protection

The old saying, 'No foot (limbs), no horse', could not be more true than when applied to an Event horse. His legs are expected to clock up many miles of hard work, and the chances of their collecting injuries, both in training and in competition, are high. Therefore a groom must be aware of what can go wrong with them and why, how best to look after them, and what to do when problems arise. Soundness is so important that nothing should be too much trouble for you when it involves the care and checking of horses' legs.

First of all, know what you are looking at. Study a diagram of the workings of the legs; have your rider or the vet actually show you on a live animal what is what – where each of the tendons and ligaments are and what a normal leg feels like (see diagram on page 162).

It will take time to become familiar with the legs of each horse in your charge, but it is something you must make into a habit if you are to do your job properly. Some horses will always be stocked-up, or have heat in certain places, and by checking them regularly you will know that this is just 'him'. But in another horse the same symptoms may be a warning signal of something starting to go wrong and it is this that you have to be aware of. So observe and make a note of every tiny little change. The reasons may not be apparent immediately, but they will build into a picture that can tell you a great deal. Again, this is just another aspect of the groom's ability to 'read' her horses and to know each one as an individual.

You should check the horses' legs first thing in the morning, after work, last thing at night, and after any fast work or competition. One of the best opportunities for checking legs is during morning and evening feeds, and you will soon find that it becomes second nature to run your hand down the legs. This also applies when you are grooming and tacking up. It is of equal importance to observe the horse at rest – maybe quietly relaxing in his stall or moving about the pasture. Much can be gleaned from his stance and movements. Does he seem to 'point' one foot while standing in his stall? This may indicate a soreness or one of a number of other problems. Is he still standing at the gate while his mates are cavorting about the place? These are all signals that further investigation is required.

So how do you check the legs? Begin by making the horse stand square; this is of great importance if you are to compare limbs accurately. Before laying a finger on the horse's legs, walk round him slowly, and using your eyes, check each limb from the front, the side, and the back. Take your time.

What do the legs look like? Are the knees flat? Are all the contours of the tendons straight and unfilled? Does each leg match as a pair with the other? Only when you are satisfied with your visual inspection should you proceed to go over each limb with your hands.

The fore legs
The tendons in the front legs are where most Event horses have problems, so they are the most precious. Always use the palm of your hand and the part where your thumb joins your hand, as this is the most sensitive to heat.

Attention to detail in another department. Here the rider and groom are carefully scrutinising a horse's legs.

Remember: you are feeling for heat, swelling, tenderness and any thorns, scratches, and surface injuries. Run your hand down the leg slowly, concentrating hard in order not to miss anything. All the time, compare with the other leg and with what you know to be normal. Go right the way down to the hoof, checking for heat there and feeling the pulse in the heel. If you find a sensitive spot, see if you get the same reaction by pressing on the corresponding place on the other leg. In this way you can check if your horse is being touchy or if there is really something wrong. However, picking up the leg and checking each tendon by pinching is a job best left to an experienced rider or groom, or to the vet.

The hind legs

Checking the hind legs is just the same, except that this time the hock is involved. Know all the places in this bony joint that will show signs of stress and where spavins and curbs can appear. Feel for the same things – heat, swelling and tenderness. And don't forget the feet! Heat in a foot can sometimes be the only sign of trouble.

Bandaging

There are basically three types of bandaging – for support (and this includes some exercise bandaging), for warmth and comfort, and for

(A) Putting on a stable bandage, which, extending from below the knee to the bend of the ankle, protects the leg and increases circulation. Start by slipping the end of the bandage under the cotton wool or wrap.
(B) Pulling the bandage away from the leg causes the pressure to be uneven and can damage the tendons.
(C) The overlap is spaced evenly, and secured with a safety pin or adhesive tape. If you use pins, the bandage must end on the outside of the leg, which may mean folding it back (as in photograph).

A

protection. For all types of bandaging or wrapping there are certain basic rules that must always be followed:

1 Never bandage too tightly – this can lead to tendon damage.
2 Even pressure is essential.
3 Always wrap counterclockwise on the two left or near-side legs and clockwise on the two right or off-side legs.
4 When securing with ties or pins never end a bandage directly over a tendon or on the inside of the leg for two reasons: (a) it can cause a pressure point on the tendon, resulting in a noticeably large localized swelling, and occasionally lameness; (b) the horse may catch the fastening with the other leg and the whole wrap may come undone.

Make sure that the pressure is even all the way down the bandage and that you prevent the cotton or padding underneath from wrinkling by always wrapping it around the horse's leg in the same direction as the bandage.

There are many different ways to wrap – where to start, how far to go, etc, – and you will find that riders have their own preferences. As long as the method includes all the above safety rules, then it really does not matter if, for instance, masking tape is preferred to Velcro. What is important is that the horse's legs are not damaged.

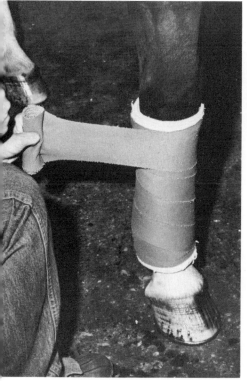
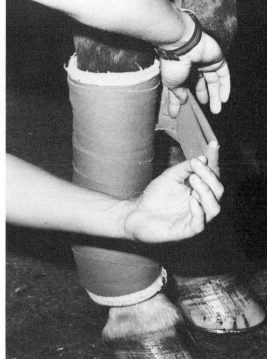

B   C

A bandage is too tight if you cannot get one or two fingers comfortably between it and the horse's leg. In the case of exercise/support bandages – which have to be tight enough to do their job effectively – you must be very careful to ensure that there is no risk of the blood supply being interfered with.

There are arguments both for and against wrapping legs regularly. Some riders prefer the legs left unwrapped, so that they will always know what is going on – bandaging may disguise other warning signs. Some will bandage all the time for warmth and for chronic fillings, such as windgalls. This is fine as long as a close eye is kept on them, so that other signs of change are not inadvertently hidden.

At competitions or when the horse is in a strange stall it is a good idea to use thick protection bandages, in case the horse rolls and knocks himself against the sides of the box, not realising that it is a different size from the one at home. Nothing would be more disappointing than to get to a Three-Day Event with a fit horse and then to end up having to withdraw because of a silly bang or cut picked up in the stall at the Event. Prevention is better than cure!

Travelling wraps are for protection and must not be too loose or too tight. There are also many excellent types of travelling boot on the market today – the only pitfall being that some of them are manufactured from

Some grooms prefer to sew the ends firmly down, as in this picture showing exercise bandages. After the bandages are secured, the surplus cotton wool is trimmed away.

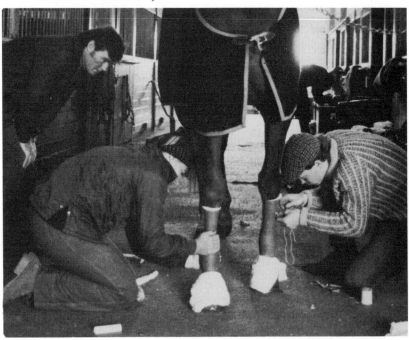

man-made materials which can cause sweating and skin irritations. So try to stick to the natural products. Travelling boots or bandages should start from the knee or hock and go right down to and over the coronet band.

When bandaging for poultices and sweats, remember that you are basically using stable bandages where there is no need for pressure. If, in the case of sweats, you also use Saran Wrap (cling film) next to the skin, apply a thin piece of cotton gauze under it. This will prevent the wrap from slipping – and thus from tightening and cutting off the blood supply. If you are applying a hot poultice, first test the temperature on your own skin, to make sure that it is not too hot.

Boots should also come into this category. They should never be too tight, and pressure should be even throughout. Remember, also, that new leather boots will often stretch, so it is a good idea to break them in before using them at an Event. Spanking new boots may look good but if half-way round a course they stretch and start to slip they can do more harm than good. In fact, they can become a possible death trap if they get caught up on something, or if a stone gets lodged between the boot and the horse's leg.

Using talcum powder on the insides of the boots before putting them on will prevent rubbing on sensitive legs. When fitting boots, before you do the straps up place them higher than they will be when they are secured, and then slide them down into position. This is far preferable to doing them half up, then deciding they are too low and wrenching them upwards against the direction of the hair! Fasten the straps so that there is equal pressure on the leg all the way down. If the boots fit half-way over the joints, make sure that the buckles are never fastened right over the middle of a joint. The lower straps may have to be fastened a hole or two looser to allow for the wider contours of the fetlock.

Jogging in hand

Jogging up each horse every day should be another part of your routine. This is something that only takes a few minutes but is worthwhile for two reasons. In the first place it is another chance to get to know your horse and to be able to recognise how sound he is normally; you thus have a standard by which to judge when you are faced with a stiff, tired horse on the night after a Three-Day Event Speed and Endurance Test. You will also see how he is standing up to his training at home. The other reason for jogging up on a regular basis is not so important, but it will help a great deal at actual Events: you will be teaching your horse to jog in hand. This is not as simple as it sounds and is definitely not something that you should expect all horses to do on the day. Some horses are naturally idle; some may need calming down.

At Three-Day Events, the usual procedure at the veterinary inspections is to walk your horse up to the panel and halt. This gives them a chance to examine the horse if they wish. Then you will be asked to walk away from them, so that they have a view of his hind action. After this, turn (always remembering to keep the horse on your right and to turn to the right) and

Jogging each horse in hand should be part of your daily routine. As well as enabling you and the horses to become proficient at jogging, it gives you a chance to check each horse's soundness.

trot back past the panel. The whole routine should be carried out with a loose rein, so that they can see if the horse moves with a steady head carriage. Any nodding or unevenness will indicate that the horse is not sound. If you have nothing to hide, then this is well and good. If they see you hanging on to the horse's head they will be suspicious and think that you are trying to hide some unevenness in the stride – in which case they will, quite rightly, ask you to trot up again. At home, where the reason for trotting up is to check that the horse is sound, a loose rein is the only certain means of determining soundness.

When jogging a horse in hand, always make sure that the horse is straight and pointing in the desired direction. You should be able to walk or trot off with the horse obediently by your side – perhaps a cluck will prompt him into the trot. All the turns should be unrushed, and the horse should pull up smoothly and calmly.

If a horse tends to be idle, ask someone to run alongside him (just behind the handler) and to tap him with a whip at the right moment. It will sharpen him up and he will soon learn what is expected of him. An impetuous horse regularly trotted up at home will soon realise that there is really nothing to get excited about – and a lead line over the nose, or a bridle, will give you enough control to get your point across. If the horse is too enthusiastic and takes off sideways, put one lead line on each side, and ask a friend to help by being on the off-side while you trot the horse up a few times. Together you will be acting as a funnel, and this will very soon cure the sideways runner. In veterinary inspections at Events you should always use a bridle, as it is a great deal smarter than a headcollar. The only exception might be if the horse has a sore mouth, in which case any direct contact may make him fuss, or indeed make him appear to be lame.

Grooming

Presumably, if you have bought this book, you will already know the basics of actually brushing a horse! Even if you are in charge of a yard, always try to groom one or two horses yourself. In this way you will always keep up with the job and it will encourage the people working under you.

Grooming achieves more than just keeping a horse clean. It stimulates the circulation, puts a real bloom on the coat by bringing the natural oils to the

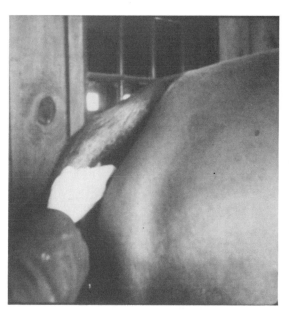

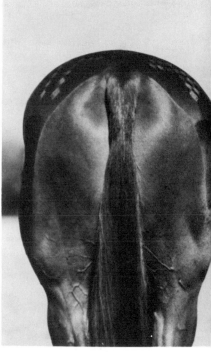

Patience and moderation are the keys to a beautifully pulled tail. Note how the hairs are removed one by one from the underneath and sides and NEVER from the top.

The pulled tail. Note how it is 'waisted' in line with the point of the buttocks. This shows the hindquarters off and also accentuates the thickness and body of the tail.

23

surface, and gives you yet another chance to get to know the horse really well – by studying all his different characteristics and all the little lumps and bumps he may have acquired.

Another essential aspect of grooming is to keep the horse looking smart. Therefore, jobs such as pulling manes and tails are very much a part of your grooming routine and should be attended to in some measure every day. Usually the job of pulling and trimming occurs at the beginning of the horse's work schedule, so it is unlikely that he will be going anywhere special until he is half-way fit. Therefore there is no need to attempt to accomplish everything in one day – it is best done a little at a time, for your horse's comfort as well as being more suited to your own routine. Once you have the manes and tails looking tidy, pulling a little every other week will be a small task and the result will be a horse with a constantly well-pulled mane and tail. Do not forget to trim the bridle path – though with fine-haired thoroughbreds this is sometimes unnecessary. Unfortunately, it seems to be the fashion to trim the whiskers around the horse's muzzle and even the eyes. If you do, you are robbing the horse of the natural 'feelers' which are there to help protect his muzzle and eyes. Lucinda Green's Regal Realm won Badminton and the World Championship with a full complement of facial whiskers, which proves that they did not impede his progress! Trim the feathers (the hair around the feet and heels) but keep in mind the protection that this hair gives and do not scalp the legs completely – just trim away the unsightly hairs. The same applies particularly to the ears, especially in the United States where there is usually a severe fly problem in the summer. It is positively cruel to remove all hairs from the ears. However, if you must trim the ears, snip away the long protruding hairs but leave the protective fine, downy hair inside the ears.

Keeping your horses looking smart and well cared for is a reflection on you – not only on your practical ability to do such things as pulling and trimming, but also on your attitude towards your job. There is so much satisfaction to be gained from seeing your horses looking neat and tidy, and all these little things add up to an overall picture of a professional and caring organisation. Nothing is more eye-catching than a well turned-out, well cared for horse . . . it will never go unnoticed.

Make sure that your equipment is always clean. There is no point at all in trying to groom a horse with a filthy brush, so make it a weekly part of your routine to wash all your grooming tools.

In the morning, after the horse has finished breakfast, begin by brushing off, or quartering – just a quick five-minute job. This entails a swift brush over the body, the removing of any stains, washing out the eyes, nose and dock, putting on a tail bandage, laying the mane over with a wet brush, and picking out and oiling the feet. This means your rider will have a smart horse to ride first thing in the morning. Again, it also gives you a chance to check that the horse has not done any damage to himself during the night. Brush off the night rugs and put on the day rugs.

Whenever you are either grooming or tacking-up, clipping, or just generally working around the horses, always keep the temperature uppermost in your mind. When you are grooming in the winter, always keep a blanket on a horse – on his hind quarters while you do the shoulders and back, and over the front when you are doing the quarters. When it is cold, get the body done and then rug the horse up before you do the head, legs and feet. It is quite unnecessary to keep the horse hanging around with no clothes on while you fiddle with some extremity that can well be tackled when the rugs are in place.

After the horse has worked, and has cooled out and dried off, you can either groom him thoroughly then or, if you intend to turn him out in the paddock, when he comes back in again. Spend as long as you need to groom him thoroughly. This may be anything from twenty minutes to an hour or more, depending really on the sort of state he is in when you get to him. Every time you groom a horse, check his legs as a matter of routine, and also pay particular attention to his feet. Check that the shoes are all still correctly fitted and that no clenches have risen. Keep an eye, also, on the wear of the shoe and the condition of the hoof itself. If your horse wears pads for protection from concussion or bruising, make sure that no foreign matter has sneaked up under the pad, or that the cushioning material that the blacksmith uses under the pad has not shifted or bunched up – both these things can cause sore and bruised feet. Use some sort of hoof dressing on the outside and inside of the feet at least once a day. This not only looks good but actually keeps the hoof moist and supple – and some dressings also act as an antiseptic that will prevent such ailments as thrush. So, be very aware of your horse's feet and make the most of the grooming time to check them.

Washing horses

In North America the weather is usually hot enough during most of the summer and autumn months to allow you to wash your horse without fear of his catching a chill. In England, hot days are few and far between, so much more care must be taken. Because Americans are so used to washing horses clean after work, the problem of catching a chill is often ignored well into the winter months and many people do not realise how quickly it can happen. If there is any doubt, a good thing to remember is to leave the head unwashed. Thirty per cent of the body heat is lost through the head, so washing it on a cool day is just asking for trouble. Once you have washed your horse, use a sweat scraper on his body and a towel for his head, body, and legs; then put a sweat sheet or cooler on him and walk him around until he is dry before putting him back into his stall. Make sure that he has dry rugs on him.

Never underestimate the value of towel rubbing – this stimulates circulation as well as drying the horse and it is something that most horses enjoy. In the winter, if you have a very wet and sweaty horse, it is a good idea just to use towels on him immediately, without even washing him, because much of the dirt will be taken off with the towel.

Always make it a practice to dry the horse's legs thoroughly, especially the heels, which are susceptible to cracking and drying. And here is a special note of warning to grooms who have charge of grey horses, or horses with white socks: pink skin is very delicate and care should be taken not to wash these areas too often or too thoroughly. The use of baby oil in the heels when the legs are dry will help to keep the skin moist, water-repellent, and supple, and will soothe any irritation.

Clipping

As the weather gets colder and your horse grows a longer coat for warmth, it may soon become necessary to clip him, according to the amount of work he is doing. This will enable him to carry out his work more comfortably. It will also make your grooming job easier, although this should never be the overriding reason. There are many different types of clip and you must choose the one best suited to the environment and the work that your horse will be doing. The following are some points to take stock of, both before and during clipping:

1 Make sure that the clippers have been serviced and are in good working order. Have the blades re-sharpened when necessary and keep them in oiled cloth to prevent rusting. Keep at least one pair of spare blades in case the initial ones become dull or accidentally chipped during the clipping process.
2 Clean the clippers often, both during and after use. The power-unit has to do a great deal of work in a season. One horse may need clipping perhaps three times each winter, and if you estimate that it takes up to two hours to clip a horse and then multiply that by ten horses, here alone you have a motor as big as your hand doing sixty hours of work! So keep the air filters clean all the time and keep the mechanism lubricated with oil to prevent the clippers from heating up too quickly. Use paraffin or kerosene to clean the blades as you work. Dip the head in, let the surplus run off and then wipe the blades dry with a rag so that none of the oil touches the horse's skin, which may lead to irritation.
3 To make life easier for you and the clippers, always try to start with a clean horse. Nothing blunts blades faster than dirt, and blunt blades will pull at the horse's hair and make him uncomfortable.
4 With a hunter clip it is helpful to mark out your lines with chalk or soap. Take the time to put the horse's saddle on him, with the girth buckled up. Then trace its outline. This will give you an accurate and even-looking finished clip.

After clipping, take a bucket of hot water, add about a pint of vinegar and, using a towel that has been wrung out in this mixture, give the horse a thorough rub all over. This will not only pick up all the little hairs that brushing may have missed, but it will also take much of the grease out of the coat and, more important, any paraffin or kerosene that may have rubbed off on to his skin. To compensate for the clipped-off hair, add an extra sheet to his usual rugs.

Try to clip on a warmish day and always keep a rug of some sort over him. Never attempt to clip a wet horse – you will not achieve a good finish and you are just asking for an electric shock.

In eventing, clipping may also take place during the summer months. At a Three-Day Event a horse needs every help to get around the cross-country course with as little strain as possible. If you had to run four miles on a hot day you would do it with the minimum amount of clothing in order to keep your body temperature down. Running with a sweater on in eighty degrees is no fun and can lead to heat stroke; it is the same with a horse galloping round a cross-country course. The only thing he has to cool him down, beside his own body system, is the wind. To give horses the best chance, many people clip them out so that the body can concentrate on the job in hand – galloping and jumping – and expend a minimum amount of effort in keeping cool. The drawback to this method is that generally a Three-Day Event is the finale of the season, and the week after the Event has ended the horse will probably be off work and on vacation – so it will be a while before you are able to turn him out in the paddock without his blankets. Also, as well as messing up his natural coat-growing cycles, you may have an added expense in that you will most probably have to feed more to compensate for the extra energy he is using in keeping himself warm. These are the pros and cons, and the decision really rests with the rider – bearing in mind the fitness of the horse, the thickness of his coat, and how hot it will be on the actual competition day. Many people feel that clipping does not help much and that a fit horse should not need such pampering.

People who do clip for Three-Day Events have the choice of either doing so before the competition starts – to give the coat a few days to settle down and lose that 'just clipped' look – or during the competition itself and, therefore, gaining the full benefit of the clip before the coat has a chance to grow back.

If you decide on the latter, it is a good idea to clip after the Dressage phase. This will mean that the horse's appearance in the Dressage arena will be enhanced by a full, unlined coat, with a natural sheen – and remember that turn-out, can earn the competitor a valuable handful of points.

Leaving the legs unclipped is always a good idea, if you are not worried about ending up with a hunter look. It is added protection – something you can never have too much of in a Three-Day Event. For the same reason – that of protection – leave the saddle patch unclipped also. Always remember that your horse's well-being and comfort take priority over appearance or fashion. When you pack to go to Events, take your clippers with you – and all the equipment that goes with them, including the paraffin, the extension wires and the adaptors. If you are travelling abroad, find out in advance if your clippers can handle the voltage. This will save turning up in a foreign country only to discover that your clippers will not work and that there are none for you to borrow.

Turning-out

The horse that we know and work with today is a long way from his natural

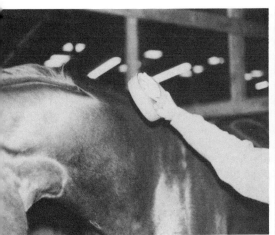 

Strapping promotes muscle tone and circulation. It should only be used on the three large muscle groups: neck, shoulders and hind quarters. Strapping is done with a folded cloth or leather strapping pad, as shown in the illustrations. Each of the three muscle groups is given a sequence of good hearty pats or bangs, following a steady and unhurried rhythm so that enough time is given for the muscle to contract and relax. It is very important for the horse to remain relaxed and not become tense.

    Begin with about 15 softer pats or bangs on each area until the horse is used to the idea. Gradually build up to a daily régime of 30 to 50 bangs on each area on both sides of the horse; the number of bangs depends on the horse's needs, level of fitness and natural condition. Strapping also stimulates natural oil secretion which results in a glossy coat, however too much strapping can cause the horse to become muscle-bound.

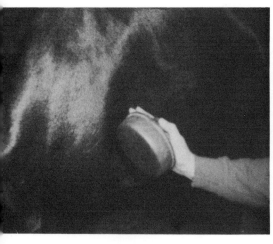 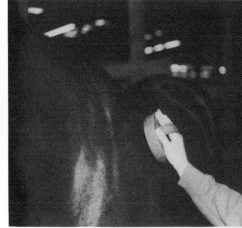

environment, in more ways than simply living in a stall instead of the great outdoors. He eats hard grains instead of a staple diet of green stuffs, and what is more this food is rationed into human-like mealtimes – in complete contradiction to nature, where he would be eating continuously. There are many ways in which we have changed the horse's life-style to suit our own needs, so we should try to adhere, as closely as possible, to the outlines that nature has set out for the horse. One of the ways in which we can do this is by turning him out to pasture as often as is practical. We tend to molly-coddle horses far too much sometimes – a little bit of mud or rain has never killed any horse in our experience and it will do their minds a world of good. The same, of course, cannot be said for your rugs or their cleanliness!

An Event horse is usually at least three-quarter bred, so in the first place you have a fairly highly strung animal to contend with. Keep him in a stall for twenty-two hours a day, feed him hard grain, and get him fit with fast work, and you will have a horse that will need frequent breaks – just to canter around and let off steam in the freedom of his own surroundings.

Make turning-out part of your routine. Make sure that your paddocks are free from holes, rubbish, poisonous plants and dangerous fencing and, ideally, have an old pony for company and safety. Often the inability of the old pony to gallop about will discourage your valuable horse from too much gallivanting around and will, therefore, prevent any accidents or strains. Make it a practice to turn horses out in boots while they are in work, at least in front – just for protection. Again, prevention is always better than cure. Check that there is a constant supply of clean drinking water available. If your field has a trough, put half a dozen goldfish in it. This will not only add colour, but the fish will keep the tank clean by eating all the little things that may grow or fall into the water.

If you intend to leave a halter on your horse while he is turned out, make sure that it is an old leather one that will break easily if he somehow manages to get it caught up on something; never turn a horse out wearing a nylon halter for this very reason. If you use New Zealand rugs that have spring clips on the leg straps, the leg straps themselves should link around each other between the hind legs; then snap them on so that the opening of the clip is against the horse. If the horse should run up against any wire fencing, this will prevent a strand of wire from getting caught in the clip, with subsequent injury to the horse. In fact, wire can cause some of the nastiest injuries to horses, so make sure that any on your land is in good safe repair and is not so low that a horse will get its legs caught in it. If you turn your horses out on a regular daily basis, the chances of them galloping about and doing themselves harm will be slim, compared to a horse that only gets out once in a while and, therefore, has plenty of energy to waste on the novelty of returning to nature.

Tack – its selection and care

One of the groom's most important responsibilities is the care of tack. This should be taken seriously and not looked upon as a tiresome task. A chain is only as strong as its weakest link, and at a Three-Day Event that link might just be part of the tack you are responsible for.

Always buy good quality leather. Cheap tack is made of cheap leather and is not worth the risk. Know how to look after it, both when it is in use and when it is stored away. Clean the tack every day. Take it apart and clean all the leather, especially where it is folded back on itself, such as where the bit hangs and where the buckles are secured.

There are many different products on the market and it is a matter of personal preference as to which one of them that you use. Personally we prefer neatsfoot oil for treating new tack and for softening old leather. If you warm the oil first, it will be absorbed faster and it will also darken new yellow tack.

A universal method which works well and which keeps the tack clean and supple is first to wash it thoroughly with warm water then to sponge it with glycerine saddle soap. If tack becomes greasy to the touch it means that it is not being cleaned thoroughly enough and has accumulated a layer of soap. To remove this residue use either a handful of soda crystals or some ammonia in the tack cleaning water.

Through cleaning your tack every day you will also have an opportunity to check its safety. Keep an eye on all the leather, all the stitching, and any non-leather parts – such as the elastic in girths and the webbing in overgirths and breastplates.

For safety's sake do not have reins re-rubbered; it is a false economy and just not worth the risk. If you cannot afford to buy a new pair of reins every time that the rubber wears away, at least keep a pair for Events only, which have not been re-rubbered. To rubber a pair of reins in the first place entails stitching down the length of the rein and across it at the ends, thus making a line of perforations in your reins. Added to these holes, new needle marks will be made when the reins are re-rubbered. As the leather under the rubber is inaccessible it never benefits from oils or soaps, so the perforations can tear as easily as a postage stamp.

Special care must be taken of the elastic and webbing parts of your tack, which will rot earlier than the leather. Sweat and rain are their worst enemies, so wash and dry them carefully. In fact, it is debatable how much benefit you will derive from having an elastic insert in a girth, as they are stretched so tight for the cross-country that the elastic becomes useless. Therefore if you can manage without them, do so. Ideally there should be three girth straps, which should be attached to two webbings going across the seat of the saddle. This ensures that your two girth buckles are never attached to the saddle on the same piece of webbing. If the webbing breaks and both buckles are on the same web, then the girth becomes unattached.

As well as inspecting your tack each day when you clean it, you should also put aside a couple of hours every month to check through everything. Include spare tack and lungeing equipment, and check all the stitch work, the strength of all the leather, and all the buckles and billets. You can afford to be rough; after all, the stress that it will have to cope with on competition days is far more than you can simulate. Bear in mind that the tack will have to stand up to the pulling and straining of a 1000-pound horse against a 165-pound load.

When buying tack it is essential to ensure that it is durable and safe. Buckles come in unbreakable metal. Stirrup leathers are now often made with reinforced pieces of either nylon or chrome leather. Stainless steel stirrups are far safer than the pliable nickel or mixed metal variety. Bits should also be made of stainless steel.

Check that the webbings in the saddles are safe and that the stitching is strong. In some saddles, the webbing is attached to the tree with tiny tacks; if this is so, it is advisable to have the saddle inspected closely to make sure that the tacks have not torn or eaten into the webbing, or that they are not so close together as to act as a perforation line. Today you can buy webbing made from unbreakable nylon. This is acceptable as long as the thread used in sewing the girth-straps down is *not* nylon as this will cut into the leather of the straps and rip them. Ask the saddler to check that the stirrup bars are safe and secure.

If your horse goes in a rubber or plastic bit, make sure that it has not been chewed and, therefore, weakened. Rubber bits should have chain or metal centres so that if the rubber breaks completely at least there is still something in the horse's mouth to provide temporary control. A lump of chain is not ideal but it is certainly better than nothing at all.

If your rider uses a weight cloth do not forget the securing straps. Check all boots worn by the horse: boot-straps probably undergo more wear and tear than any other piece of leather equipment. They are constantly getting wet, being dried out and then getting filthy again.

Never neglect the repairs. The minute that stitching starts to come adrift, have it mended. It will be cheaper than replacing the article and far safer than waiting until it breaks.

Spare tack, as opposed to the special tack kept for competition only, has to be in good shape, too. You may need it on cross-country day for emergency breaks.

For your own peace of mind, make sure that *all* the tack is in good shape. It is as much part of the groom's job as looking after the horses, and just as important in the run-up to the Events as the fitness work. There is a great deal of satisfaction to be had from a clean and sparkling bridle and from the knowledge that it is safe to do its job.

Finally, make sure that all the tack fits correctly and that each horse has a bridle that is his own and that really fits him. Nothing looks worse, or is more annoying to the horse, than a bit that is hanging out of his mouth, a drop noseband that is interfering with his breathing, or a saddle pad that is too small and badly arranged on his back. Check that the browband is long enough – is it comfortable for the horse or is it pinching his ears? Do the buckles of the noseband and cheek pieces lie comfortably half-way down the cheek bone, or do they sit up around the base of the ears, poking into the horse's skin? Are the buckles on the noseband fastened in such a way that they catch the sensitive skin of the underside of the jaw, or are they positioned correctly so as not to pinch the skin over a bony protrusion? Are you able to fit two fingers above the cavesson noseband and the edge of

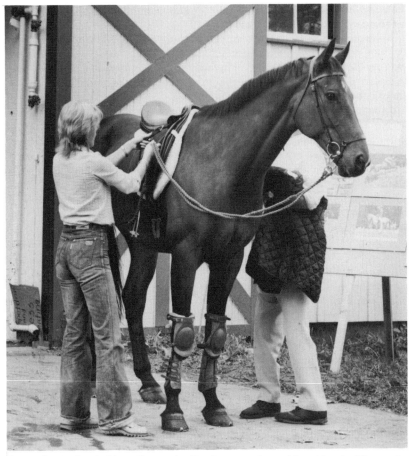

Preparing to hack. Note the protective knee pads and front boots. The pads are essential for safety when riding on the roads.

the cheek bone, or is it so high that it is rubbing against the bone? Is the bit so low that it is hitting the horse's teeth, or so high that you cannot fit a finger between the bit and the corner of the mouth?

The saddle, also, should come under just as much careful scrutiny. Make sure that the arch is high enough off the horse's back so that even when you are on him you can still get at least three fingers under the front arch. Saddle pads must fit and must extend at least two inches beyond the back of the saddle. If the edge of the pad coincides with the edge of the saddle, then a pressure point may develop. Always pull the pad right up into the arch of the saddle before you tighten up the girth. If you fail to do this, the pad will pull down across the withers, causing severe discomfort and pressure sores.

If you take the time to fit everything correctly on the horse you will avoid unnecessary injuries that result from badly-fitting tack. The result will also be pleasing to the eye and will show how much you know and care.

If your rider can afford it, it is worth keeping a set of good tack just for Events. This enables you to keep the tack as smart as possible and also reassures you that it is safe, because it is not in use every day all the year round. If you are able to do this, bring the special tack out at least once a month and oil it to prevent it from drying out. Make sure, also, that it is not stored in a damp place, where mildew may cause it to rot.

Safety

Safety should be an all-important factor in any equestrian establishment. Everything you do must be carried out safely as well as efficiently. If there is a risk that either the horse, the rider, or yourself will be hurt, you have failed in your job. Set standards and stick to them. Even if some procedures take extra time, they are never wasted in your battle to cut out all possible risks. Make sure that your yard is a safe place to work in, that all electrical appliances are checked regularly and are not accessible to horses.

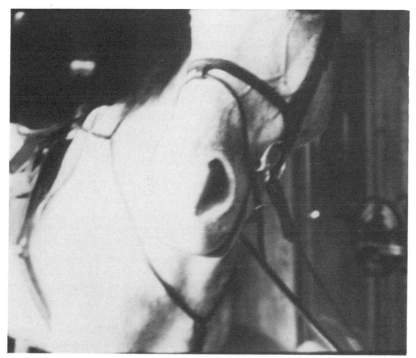

After exercise, having loosened the lower strap of a flash or cross noseband, always secure the buckle on a looser hole so that if the horse shakes his head there will be no chance of the sharp metal buckle hitting either the horse or the groom in the eye. It will also prevent the loss of the flash strap.

Safety is also a vital factor in your work around the yard. Even if you know the horses well enough to trust them to stand without being tied up, it is always possible that some stupid little unexpected thing may happen to spook a fit and valuable horse.

Discipline your horses so that they have respect for you and know their place. If they have to be tied for you to work in the stall, then tie them. Never let them lean over the wheelbarrow when you muck out – they just might try to climb out and cause all kinds of problems. If you have rings in the walls, or tethering points in your van or trailer, attach pieces of string to them, ready for tying up the horses. If a horse panics, the string will break easily, a metal fixture will not. NEVER tie a horse to bars on the stall, or to temporary stabling, without using the string or baling twine; and NEVER tie a horse to a jump standard, brush box, door or anything movable that could come away with a panic-stricken horse and cause severe injuries.

Make sure that your yard is safe. Stable doors should be wide enough to allow a horse to walk through without the danger of banging his hips. The windows should have bars, or be high enough to prevent the horse from breaking the glass with either his nose or his heels. Always have enough bedding, so that he can roll without scraping his hocks or knees on the floor. Keep thick banks or walls of bedding up around the sides to stop draughts and to prevent the horse from becoming cast if he rolls too close to the walls. A generous amount of bedding, whether it be straw, shavings or peat, is no waste of money. In England, where floors are mostly concrete, it is essential to have plenty of bedding to keep out the cold, to prevent grazes and to encourage the horse to rest. If you have a dirt floor, the problem is not so great, but you must keep the bedding thick and inviting at all times. This also means keeping it clean. It will be wasted if it is not handled correctly. Even a deep-litter bed can work perfectly well if it is cared for often and conscientiously. So ask yourself – if you were a horse, would you want to lie down in one of your stables?

Deep-litter bedding

This way of bedding is particularly suitable with sawdust or shavings, but it can also be used with straw. The manure should be removed from the stable each day, but a good amount of the wet material underneath should be left to build up, so that the bedding could be up to a foot deep. There are several advantages with this method. Once the bed is established you need only add a small amount of bedding each day. This will ensure that the horse has a comfortable surface to lie on, as there are no bare spots. When used in a stall with an old, uneven clay floor, the wet bedding will fill in the holes, allowing a level area for the horse's comfort. It will provide warmth during the winter months. Lastly – although certainly not the only reason for employing this method – it is less time-consuming than the traditional way of mucking out. When starting a deep-litter bed, work by these rules:

1 Begin with plenty of bedding.
2 Keep the bed level at all times.

3 Remember that, no matter which system you use, a horse should be able to walk and lay ON TOP of the bedding and not through it. It is a common mistake to fluff up the bedding material instead of laying it down firm and level. If the bedding is fluffed up it is easily kicked about and the horse will more than likely end up standing or laying on a bare floor.
4 Since wet spots appear as mounds in the deep-litter bed, remove enough of the soiled bedding until you once again have a level surface.

Make sure that the doors are secure and that any equine 'Houdini' cannot reach the latches. If you are lucky enough to have a wash stall, make sure that it has a mat of coconut or serrated rubber – something that will stop the horses from slipping when the floor is wet.

If you use cross ties, see that they have quick-release snaps on them, in case a horse pulls back in fright and cannot get loose without the risk of really hurting himself. Make sure that the cross ties are not of the chain variety, unless they are covered with tubing; horses who play with the cross ties may get their teeth caught in the links, and may panic.

Always use a lead rope when you are leading a horse around. This is a fairly obvious point to make, but sometimes it may seem a waste of time fitting a proper halter and lead shank just to lead a horse from one stall to the other. However, if you take the easy way out something untoward may happen; you will lose control and end up feeling a real idiot.

When out hacking or exercising, try to make it a habit to have boots on the horse for protection, and put knee pads on him when you are doing road work.

When you are away at Events, there is always some time during the day when you will find yourself grazing a horse, or just leading him about, and this is a tempting opportunity to have a gossip with someone doing the same job as yourself. But remember not to get too close or to allow the horses to nuzzle each other – this can lead to a swift and very unwanted kick. Use your common sense. Think ahead. And try not to cut any corners that may leave you wide open to accidents.

Feeding

Feeding horses is an art, and there are a few basic rules to follow – such as, feed little and often; increase or decrease quantities gradually; always use good quality foodstuffs; always water before feeding; never feed directly before exercise; and always cut down the protein and carbohydrates, while increasing the roughage or bulk intake of a resting horse. This is the structure within which to work. From here on it is up to you and your rider to discover the needs and the tastes of each horse as an individual, so that you can give each one exactly what he needs to do his work well, to build up muscle and to be kept happy.

In this part of the job the groom has the advantage over the rider, as you are the one who will actually be feeding the horse. You will see how enthusiastic he is for his meals, what he does not like, and whether he could eat more if it was given to him. You will develop an eye that will see every change in his waist line. In turn, the rider will be able to tell from riding him if he lacks energy and needs more oats – or if he is finding the fitness work too hard because he is carrying excess weight.

So between you, you should be able to build up a fairly accurate picture of each horse's nutritional needs. Start off with a big, clear feed chart in the feed room. Keep an up-to-date record of each horse's feeds and note in your diary any changes. When you go away to Events, do remember to copy each chart to take with you. Do not leave it to memory.

Make the washing out of feed buckets and water buckets a daily routine. It is unhygienic and sloppy to neglect this, and highly sensitive thoroughbreds can be easily put off their grain and water if the containers smell stale. This also applies to automatic water bowls. They collect just as much dirt as a bucket and can be damaged if silt and grain are allowed to build up in the mechanism.

Make sure that all your feed grains are fresh and wholesome. You really have no idea how long your feed merchant has kept the feed stored, so only order enough to last you a maximum of two weeks. Remember that grains, such as oats, that have been cracked or rolled, only have a lifetime of about ten days before they lose their protein and therefore their feeding value.

Sometimes it is possible to buy grain in bulk. In such cases, ask the feed merchant to store it and then roll or crush small amounts at a time and deliver them to you on a regular basis. This is an excellent idea if you can afford the initial outlay, as it will ensure a consistency in quality and in protein and mineral counts. Many people send samples off to be analysed, which is well worth doing when you are looking for good grain. The better the quality, the better the horse will be.

If you travel abroad with your horses, you will quite often find that you are not allowed to take grain and pellets with you. You are therefore going to have your work cut out trying to simulate his diet with strange foodstuffs. In these instances, always take with you the analysis tags from the bags at home, so that you can match them when you arrive at the Event and can try to get the closest form of feed content that your horse is used to. Avoid trying out all the strange and varied feed varieties that you can find abroad. It is foolish and if your horse becomes sick it may well wreck your chances in the competition.

If your horse is a fussy eater or goes off his feed almost completely at Events be flexible and resourceful but stick mainly to what you are used to. Entice him to eat by mixing in apples and carrots and by giving him only tiny feeds at frequent intervals so that he is never overfaced but takes just enough to whet his appetite.

Keep all the feed mangers and buckets clean, all the measures accurate, and all the feed times on a routine basis – three or four times a day. Most horses eat better last thing at night, in the peace and quiet. So start the day off with a small feed – particularly as you will be exercising during the morning. Then the rest of the meals can be progressively larger.

It seems to have become almost a fashion to provide some sort of additive or feed supplement. There are excellent brands on the market which contain a variety of minerals and vitamins that the horse may be lacking. But beware. You can really upset the horse's natural internal balance if you overdo it. Salt should be a regular additive; a tablespoon in the evening feed will help the horse, especially if he is in work, by replacing some of the minerals lost through sweating. Electrolytes are also a special form of additive specifically for this purpose. Used extensively in the United States and in other hot countries, they have recently been introduced in England, but because the climate is usually so mild they are only necessary during Events and in really hot weather, when the horse will be losing a lot of body salts. It is wasteful to feed them when the horse is not working too hard or during cold weather. As a horse's body cannot store the salts they pass right through him, so it is a case of money down the drain.

If the horse is getting good quality feed and hay; if he has access to grass; and if his feed rations are well balanced and appropriate to his size, age, and work, additives should not strictly be necessary. If you think that your horse is a little under par, ask your vet to give him a blood test. This will determine if he is lacking in anything: he could perhaps be slightly anaemic, which is often the case with horses that are working hard. A horse undergoing regular, intensive work is not in his natural state. So, if necessary, by all means use additives – but be careful not to use too many.

Bran and boiled feeds should be a part of any good groom's régime. They are well-tried and long established feeding methods and are very beneficial to the horse for many reasons.

A bran mash is basically bran and hot water – very basic and perhaps not very mouth-watering. To this can be added a couple of pounds of oats, or even some apple or carrot slices to make it more interesting. Allow three pounds of bran per horse. Put it in a bucket and pour over it enough boiling water to soak the bran until it is the consistency of a very sloppy cake mix. Cover the bucket with an old hessian or jute sack – or anything else that will act as insulation – and let it stand for fifteen minutes. By then you will find that the bran has absorbed all the water and is of a crumbly consistency and still warm. Add whatever you wish to make a delicious meal for your horse.

The mash should be fed at least once a week, ideally on the night before the horse's rest day. A bran mash fulfils a number of purposes. As it lacks the protein that a horse's normal feed contains, it prevents the legs from stocking-up because of over-feeding on a rest day. It also helps to prevent the tieing-up that often happens to horses after a day off when they have been kept on full rations. Bran is also a natural source of selenium, the essential mineral that is today so often used to prevent and treat tieing-up.

Bran mashes also have a laxative quality so they help to prevent constipation, which in turn can lead to colic – a blockage caused by a diet of hard food and man-made water-absorbing pellets. This problem increases as the horse ages, so older horses will benefit greatly from a couple of mashes every week.

It is ideal if you can include a pound of damp bran in every evening feed, as well as a bi-weekly mash. Bran is excellent for a horse with a sore mouth. It is also a first-rate drawing agent and can be used when poulticing feet.

Many people give boiled feedstuffs. This is an excellent way of warming a horse up, putting weight on a skinny horse and giving him a meal that will not overload him with protein. It may be used in the same way as bran, the night before a rest day. Boiled feed is a great filler, and because most of the energy value has been boiled away, the grains are no longer of the same protein count as their dry-fed counterparts.

The three main grains are whole oats, whole barley, and linseed or flax seeds. Do not use crushed or rolled grains, as this will give a porridge-like consistency. All three should be soaked before they are boiled. Allow a pound of grain per horse before boiling, and soak for a minimum of four hours. In the case of linseed it is safer to leave it immersed in water overnight. If the kernels have not cracked during the cooking and the linseed is therefore not thoroughly cooked, you run the risk of poisoning your horse. Boil the grain with at least a couple of inches of water covering it for thirty minutes to one hour and then simmer until cooked – about three hours. You can test that the grain is cooked by examining a kernel and ensuring that the husk has cracked and the hull is cooked. With the linseed, when the kernel cracks, the juices mix with the water to form a thick, sticky soup – this is good. With boiled feeds add a couple of pounds of bran.

Always ensure that bran mashes and boiled feeds have cooled down sufficiently for the horse to be able to eat them comfortably. Horses are not naturally used to eating heated foodstuffs. A useful point to remember is that linseed contains an oil that will bring a shine to any coat.

A final note on feeding. Nowadays one can buy sugarbeet cubes and sugarbeet meal, as well as alfalfa cubes. These feedstuffs must be soaked in water and allowed to fully absorb as much liquid as possible. If they are fed dry they will start to absorb body fluids and will expand in the horse's stomach – cubes can double or triple their size. This will lead to all sorts of intestinal trouble. If you fed a scoop of dried sugarbeet pulp to your horse, once it had absorbed enough water it would be equivalent to two or three scoops – and what a belly ache that could cause! So allow plenty of water and at least an hour or two for such dried feeds to soak before feeding.

Hay is just as important as feed. There are many kinds available, and they differ from place to place. Some (eg alfalfa) are richer than others, and must be modified with the correct quantity and quality of grain, so that your horse's intake is well balanced.

Any hay that you buy should smell sweet and undusty. It should be crisp to the touch, unless it is meadow hay with less goodness, which is soft. It should be greenish-brown in colour and should have flower heads that are open but still intact – which will prove that it was cut at the right time. If there are no heads it means that the grass was allowed to go to seed before it was cut and therefore is of less nutritional value. It should not contain any weeds or thistles, and all the bales in a load should be of the same quality.

Because the quality and the contents of hay differ considerably from one load to another it is desirable to buy a large load at one time, to ensure that your horse is getting the same amount of goodness and protein throughout his training in any given season. This may sound ultra picky, but a change of hay just before a competition can really upset a sensitive horse's metabolism. So at the beginning of each season, work out roughly the amount you will need to carry you through to the end – and then make sure that you have enough good, dry and well-ventilated storage space to accommodate four or five tons of hay.

Now and again, if it has been a bad year for hay or if it is the wrong time of year to obtain really good hay, you might find yourself having to buy a load that is a little dry or dusty. In this case, if you have a horse with a wind problem or a chronic cough the hay should be totally immersed in water for a couple of hours to eliminate the dust. It will also make the hay more palatable, for you will, in effect, be re-constituting it back to a grass-type feed. The water you are left with is like a tea – which the horses will enjoy. It will have some goodness in it and all the dust and grit will have sunk to the bottom of whatever container you are using. Try this method before totally eliminating hay from a coughing horse's diet; with eight out of ten horses it will solve the problem. A plastic dustbin is an ideal container and is light enough to be taken away with you, whilst also acting as another receptacle in which to pack gear.

Hay stimulates the digestive tract, thus enabling the horse to break down more efficiently the grain that is fed later, so the horse should be allowed some hay to munch before his feed. The quantities of hay given first thing in the morning and at noon should be smaller than that at night.

Veterinary care

In any yard it is advisable to have a well-stocked and comprehensive medicine chest. It should contain all the basics, such as thermometers, scissors, tweezers, cotton pads, bandages, Vaseline, and iodine. Also included should be a tourniquet, with instructions on how to use it; a colic medicine and a drench bottle; some sort of general antiseptic cream, powder and spray; Epsom Salts (which can be used for many purposes); hypodermic needles and syringes (but you must know how to use them); and a reliable antibiotic, in case you need to administer some quickly because the vet is not immediately available. It is also advisable to invest in a pair of hoof testers and a basic farrier's kit. With these tools you will be able to test a lame horse's foot for bruising or other damage, and you, yourself, will be able to remove a dangerously spread shoe immediately, without having to call on the blacksmith.

Each yard has its own remedies and preferred medications, the scope of which will depend on the needs of your horses and your experience as a groom in handling them. Make sure that any type of injections are stored at the recommended temperature, and that they are fresh (the expiry date is always printed on the vials). Make sure, too, that each bottle of medication is clearly marked and that the instructions are noted on them. If you know that a particular horse reacts badly to a certain medicine – for example, many horses are allergic to penicillin – make sure that everyone knows and that a note of it is clearly written somewhere inside the medicine chest.

As well as a medicine supply at home, you should always have one that travels with the horses. When you are away at a competition but have left some horses at home, both camps must have an emergency kit on hand. Also, you should always have the vet's telephone number, both at home and at work, pinned up near or on the medicine chest.

In our sport as in many others, certain drugs and substances are illegal during competition. Make sure that any medication which you are giving your horse is not on the banned list. Some drugs can stay in the blood-stream for days, or even weeks, after the treatment has actually been given, so find out from your vet if anything you are using needs to be discontinued weeks or days in advance. Your horses are quite likely to be given a blood test at some time during an Event, and any trace of a forbidden substance means elimination. It is surprising how many harmless medications for topical use contain banned substances. For instance, the cream that you are using for scratches may not be safe. The fact that the horse is not actually eating the preparation does not mean that it has not been absorbed into his blood-stream. Remember that the skin absorbs creams and other such preparations and they *do* enter the blood-stream. There was a case in England a few years ago in which a horse was blood tested during an Event and the analysis was positive. All the rider had done was to apply some antiseptic and healing cream on a small over-reach. But the cream happened to contain a forbidden substance . . . which resulted in elimination. So if you are in doubt, check with your vet before using any preparation. Though these rules do not apply at some local Events, they are strictly enforced at all international Events and at some of the larger national competitions. So make a point of studying all the rules. Keep up-to-date with any changes. And never think that you can avoid getting caught. It just is not worth it.

No one is of greater value to you and your horse than a good veterinary surgeon. They are worth their weight in gold. But remember that they are busy people and that you are only one among many clients. A good vet will be able to get to know each horse in your yard as the years go by and, in turn, will be able to treat any illness or lameness with an accumulation of knowledge and insight into each horse's individual needs.

After a horse has been turned out for his holiday and you bring him up to begin work, it is in everyone's interest to see that he is well, right from the start. All horses suffer from parasites of some kind and in varying degrees of severity, depending on the quality of the pasture that they have been living on and the care that they have received in the past. So start the season by having your horse wormed. After this, have him wormed on a regular basis – every six to eight weeks. If at any time you suspect that he is not as well as he could be, do a worm count. Also alternate your worming medicine, so that the worms do not become immune to one particular type. Always talk this over with your vet, as he may be able to suggest a brand that will help you, or he will tell you what type of worms are prevalent at a particular time of year. Write the worming dates in your diary and calculate if any of them are going to clash with any Events or fast work. After a horse is wormed he really should have a couple of days off, or at least do only very light work. Worming can put a horse slightly under the weather, so it would be unfair and perhaps detrimental to your horse's well-being if you wormed him just before a bout of hard work.

Teeth are something that many people overlook and they are a subject that needs to be discussed, for the correct care can help your rider as well as your horse. In the wild, horses live on soft green vegetation, so the teeth never get undue wear and tear. In the environment in which we put them they are expected to live on hard grain, which wears the teeth at an incredibly fast rate. If the teeth are allowed to go unattended they will form sharp edges and uneven surfaces that will make eating hard work for the horse, resulting in wasted grain. They may also cut the horse's mouth and make riding difficult: the bit pulls the cheeks and tongue on to the rough edges and cuts them. This makes the horse sore and fussy in his mouth and may impede his progress in training. So it is wise to have the teeth checked at least twice a year, which is best done at the start of each season. Most equine vets will deal with your horses' teeth for you, but there are also a number of people who specialise in horse dentistry. Be influenced by their reputation and by reliable hearsay – as in any profession there are the goodies and the baddies! When the vet or the dentist checks and floats the teeth he will also be able to remove any loose milk teeth or wolf teeth that may be causing discomfort.

Horses need protection against tetanus and influenza, just as humans do. So make sure that each horse is up-to-date with his inoculations. As with worming, giving a horse a 'flu injection should be timed so that it does not coincide with work. Depending on the type of serum that is used – and your vet will be able to advise you on this – the horse should have an easy work schedule following a 'flu injection. Any fast work directly after such medication can seriously damage a horse's system and may result in heart or lung strain.

It seems that more people give intravenous injections themselves in America than they do in England. Most people leave it to the vet – which is preferable. It is a risky thing to attempt if you are not totally sure of what you are doing or if you are unaware of how much damage you can cause. Air let into a main vein can kill a horse, and if serum escapes it can affect the walls of the vein and cause irritation and permanent damage. Intra-muscular injections are easier and much safer and are something that every groom should know how to do. Ask the vet to show you how to give them, so that if ever one of your horses needs a shot of antibiotics and the vet is unable to attend, you will be able to help the horse to some extent.

Always use new and sterile needles and syringes. It really is not worth risking infection by boiling syringes and re-using them. They only cost a few pennies and – rather than having a horse out of action because of a blood infection – it is worth throwing them away after a single use.

There are three main places where intra-muscular injections may be given – in the neck, in the chest, and in the rump. Although the easiest place is the neck, most people in the eventing world prefer the chest – in case the horse reacts to the injection, causing a swelling to appear. If a swelling occurs in the neck it may interfere with the horse's flexion, whereas a swelling between the legs will not affect him so badly.

When administering an injection, clean the area thoroughly with an alcohol swab, insert the needle and gently pull back on the syringe plunger. If the syringe fills with blood you know you have hit a vein and you should then try again. You will know that you are into the muscle if when you retract the syringe tube there is nothing but a vacuum of air. Push the fluid slowly into the muscle and then swiftly remove the needle. Wipe again with the swab, and check that there is no undue bleeding.

Shoeing

A good blacksmith is an essential member of your team. Be on good terms with him and realise that he is as busy as the vet. Try to make his life easier by always booking him well in advance and being there when he arrives, so that you can help him with the horses; and tell him what type of shoes each horse will need.

Most Event horses will need studs or screws in their shoes at Events, to prevent slipping. After the blacksmith has made the holes, plug them up with cotton wadding that has been soaked in oil or Vaseline, to keep the thread from being damaged by dirt or grit. This will also make your job easier when it comes to putting in the studs.

There is no set time at which your horse should be shod, other than when his feet need trimming or when the shoes need replacing. It is no good thinking that you will have him shod once every six weeks, because each horse is different. It will depend on how quickly his feet grow, what surface you are working him on, and when the Events are scheduled. Ideally, you should have a horse shod about three days before he is to compete. This will mean that he will have new tight-fitting shoes at the Event, thus eradicating the chance of losing a shoe. It will also give him time enough to get used to them. Going to Events with shoes that are hanging off, or have no tread left, is just asking for trouble. Remember that at the beginning of the season your horse will probably be doing a great deal of slow work on the roads, which will wear the shoes down quickly. So ask the blacksmith to put borium or solder on the shoes to give them more wear.

If you are clever and know how each horse wears his shoes, you can work from the diary. If you calculate back from the Events that he will be competing in, you can roughly estimate when the blacksmith will be needed. This will not only help your blacksmith to plan his own work schedule, but if you are able to book him in advance you will better guarantee that he will be there when you need him. Also, remember that each horse that is competing should have a spare set of shoes with him at the Events. Thus if he needs to have a shoe replaced quickly you already have some that are made for him and that fit – which will save a great deal of wasted time. Ask your blacksmith to make the shoes up, and to fit them to your horse, so that you are sure they are the correct size. Horses' feet change all the time, so whenever you go to an Event ask the blacksmith to check that the spare shoes are still the correct size and shape. They might

The blacksmith plays an important part in the running of an efficient yard.

need some alterations, as they may have been unused for a year or more.

Keeping a close watch on the shoe situation is a task for a meticulous groom with an eye for detail. Each horse should have his shoes checked each day to make sure that they have not started to spread, and that there are no risen clenches. This check should become second nature to you and it is something that can be done when you check the legs and when you are grooming. Always be thinking of the future – what competitions are coming up, what type of work the horse will be doing, and how much notice to give the blacksmith.

Watch how the horse moves. Often little problems, such as interfering or tripping, can be rectified by the blacksmith with special shoeing – but he will only be able to do this if you give him the relevant information. Always trot the horse out after he has been shod, just to check that he has not been shod too tightly or that he has not been pricked. No-one is perfect – a blacksmith will not make a mistake intentionally, and he will be only too glad to rectify any errors.

We have now covered all the basics that are part of an Event groom's life and work at home. The importance of keeping everything organised cannot be stressed too often. It will make your life much easier when the season gets under way and when there is little time for searching for things that you have misplaced.

Keep all the horse clothing clean and in good repair and all the show rugs clean and ready to go – it should just be a matter of opening a cupboard and loading all the necessary equipment. Try to keep the place clean and tidy: it will be a reflection of your attitude towards your job. A clean, tidy and efficient yard is something to be proud of and is so much more pleasant to work in.

Equipment guide

The following is a fairly comprehensive list of equipment that you will need for a Three-Day Event horse. Obviously there may be items that you will not need or own; or perhaps you have a few items of your own that are not listed here. Whatever the case, this is just a guideline for anyone who is likely to pack for a Three-Day Event. It can also be adapted for One-Day Events, omitting anything superfluous. In some instances the items mentioned may be ideal things to own but financially unrealistic. Don't worry. Your Three-Day Event will not be a disaster just because you do not have everything that is listed. Pick what you think is necessary or helpful to you and add to it, or substitute. This is only a guide, not an order.

When you make lists you may find it helpful to start at the lower end of the horse. In this way you will be able to envisage everything you need, and be less likely to forget something.

If you can keep the tack in a separate trunk it will stay cleaner and will be more easily accessible. We presume that your rider will take care of such items as whips, spurs and hats.

ALL ITEMS SHOULD BE CLEARLY LABELLED WITH INITIALS
TACK

Bridles (complete for dressage, cross-country and show jumping)

One spare bridle (for cross-country day, can be dressage bridle)

Assortment of bits if change is likely

Bootlace (to tie bridle into plait on cross-country day)

Martingale and spare, if used

Breastplate/girth and spare

Spare pair of rubber reins with martingale stops, if used

Dressage saddle, stirrups, leathers and girth

Jumping saddle, stirrups, leathers and girth

Spare girth that fits jumping saddle

Overgirth and spare

Weight cloth and lead

Assortment of every-day and show saddle pads

Spare stirrup and leather (can be from dressage saddle)

Lungeing cavesson

Lunge whip
Lunge line
Side reins
Good headcollar and lead shank
Spare headcollar and lead shank

Tack cleaning equipment
Metal polish
Bridle hook and saddle horse
Two pairs of hole punchers

BOOTS AND BANDAGES

Two pairs of over-reach/bell boots
Every-day exercise boots (all round)
Boots or bandages for cross-country
Boots or bandages for show jumping
One pair of spare front boots for cross-country
One pair of spare back boots for cross-country

Tail bandages
Travelling bandages and boots
Assortment of leg bandages and cottons/gamgee
Poultice paper and bandages
Plastic wrap (cling film) for leg sweats
Talcum powder for inside of boots to prevent rubbing
Pins and tape for securing wraps

BLANKETS

All the horse's night blankets
Two anti-sweat sheets
One cotton sheet
One cooler
One waterproof sheet

One quarter sheet
One good day rug for show
Appropriate rollers and wither pads

WASHING-DOWN EQUIPMENT

Three or four washing-down buckets
Sponges, shampoo
Two scrapers
At least eight towels
A body brace for the water

Blueing for grey horses
Hose and/or whirlpool boots
Water containers (preferably thermal)
Portable heating element (will heat a bucket of water quickly)

STUD BOX containing:

Assortment of different-sized studs
Tap for making the thread in a stud hole
Wrench for screwing in studs
Awl or nail for picking out the packing and dirt
Spare shoes and pads

Packing – cotton wool and oil/Vaseline to protect stud holes
Toothbrush for cleaning studs
Easyboot and Elastoplast (if a shoe comes off on steeplechase)
Blacksmith's tools
Hoof pick

NUTRIENTS

Feed and hay (include bran)
Feed and water buckets
Feed chart and scoop

Additives, salt, electrolytes
Apples and carrots
Haynet

45

STABLE EQUIPMENT

Bedding (if not supplied by Event organization)
Muck skep and mucking-out tools
A muzzle (to stop horse eating bedding)
Disinfectant
Stall guards (where protection is inadequate or there are no doors)
Tool box (screw eyes, snaps, nails, hammer, electrical tape, etc.)

GROOMING KIT AND SPECIAL ITEMS

Grooming kit
Grooming halter
Fly spray
Hoof pick and hoof dressing
Plaiting (braiding) equipment
Clippers, extension cord, oil and blades
Twitch
Paper, pens and thumb tacks
Grease or equivalent, and rubber gloves
Detergent to remove grease
Leg braces and poultices
Thermometer (take horse's temperature daily)
Two pairs of scissors
Flashlight with good batteries
Poll guard

FIRST-AID CHEST FOR THE HORSE with such items as:

Second thermometer
Gauze pads and gamgee
Two Ace bandages, tape and pins
One spider bandage
One instant ice pack
Scissors and tweezers
Big syringe for dousing wounds
Antiseptic cream
Antiseptic powder
Antiseptic liquid soap
Iodine *or* peroxide for diluting and using as a wash
Epsom salts (for soaking sore feet and as a laxative)
Sodium bicarbonate (added to feed can help prevent tieing up, dissolved in water is a soothing wash for skin rashes)

Calamine (for irritations)
Witch hazel astringent and cooling agent (for sore backs, etc.)
Vaseline
Glycerine ointment (used with cling film to induce sweating)
Mineral oil (as a colic drench)
Colic drench/Milk of Magnesia
Drenching bottle/syringe
Aspirin
Clotting powder and tourniquet (both to stop profuse bleeding)

One small first-aid kit for humans
A second smaller first-aid kit to go to the Steeplechase

Competitor's Event Check List

14 Weeks Before Event

Plan and commit to paper a progressive and day-by-day work programme for your horse that will have him as fit, healthy and prepared for the Event as possible.

Have horse's teeth checked and floated.

Have a blood sample tested to ensure that all is well from the start.

Worm horse with appropriate worming medicine.

Book the blacksmith.

Check the horse is up-to-date with all the necessary vaccinations:
Tetanus Toxoid, Eastern Western Encephomyelitis, Venezuelan Equine
Encephalitis, Influenza. (The Influenza vaccination has a relatively short life
span compared to the other vaccinations, which are administered annually.
The Influenza vaccination can be given every three months if deemed
necessary.)
Check that you have a recent negative Coggins test certificate (EIA-Equine
Infectious Anaemia). Make copies to be sent in with all entries.
Make a thorough examination of all equipment.
Ensure that horse van, truck and trailer are checked and serviced.

6 Weeks Before Event
Mail entry (enclose fee, copy of Coggins certificate and any stabling
requests).
Organise someone to groom for you at the Event, and someone to look after
any horses left at home.
Make accommodation arrangements for yourself and your groom.
Confirm transport for horse (if not your own); van or trailer should be clean
and in good running order; check oil, brakes and tyres.
Get spare set of shoes made and pads cut if used.
Make a thorough examination of all tack and equipment and get repairs
done now and purchase any new equipment required (new tack should be
well broken in and given time to stretch before ever being used in competition).
Paint buckets, trunks, stable tools, etc. Label all equipment.
Get a blood sample tested to check that the horse is healthy and is handling
the progressively harder work well. A test at this point in the training
programme can often catch a hint of the beginnings of anaemia – a condition
due to hard work and a lack of appropriate and necessary nutrients – long
before signs are physically noticeable.

1 to 2 Weeks Before Event
Complete finishing touches to pulled mane and tail, clip if appropriate.
Make a thorough examination of all tack and equipment.
Re-shoe horse for Event with all necessary stud holes or caulks; ask black-
smith to check that spare set of shoes is still correct size.
Get a blood sample tested to ensure that the horse is definitely in tip-top
condition.
Make sure you have all necessary items for first-aid kits and any special
items such as poultice, etc. Check that all medicines are not out of date.
Clean brushes, rugs, saddle pads, wraps, etc.
Organise your own clothes and competition apparel. Dry clean, mend,
polish.
KNOW the Rule Book; make sure you have learned correct dressage test.
Confirm any hotel reservations; double-check any special stabling requests.

Shipping Equipment
Up-to-date maps; directions to Event, stabling and hotel; telephone
numbers for all three.

Omnibus, Rule Book, address book.
Major credit card, plenty of loose change.
Good spare tyre. Check that jack is complete, in good working order, and that you know how and where to work it.
Flares.
Headcollar with protective fuzzies and rope shank.
Spare headcollar and lead shank for inside cab of truck/van.
Shipping boots and bandages, tail wrap and tail guard, surcingle and pad.
Head bumper/poll guard.
Full haynet.
Water bucket and full water container.
Anti-sweat sheet, sheet or rug depending on weather.
Accessible first-aid kit.
Lunge line.
Broom.

You will notice that the medical kit is very basic, as we realise that everyone has their personal preferences or potions that they use. Obviously you will need to select or discard as necessary.

Out of all this equipment you will need items to take to the 'box'. The choice is up to you. You will need any spare tack that you may have, plus

The well-prepared Event horse. Note the healthy coat, good muscle-tone, tight legs, and eager expression.

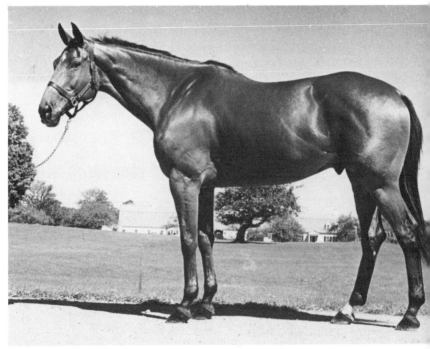

washing-down equipment and some sheets for the horse. In addition you will need some sort of medical equipment, although there are vets available with their own supplies. At the Steeplechase you will need a small bucket with the Easyboot (or shoes if there is a blacksmith there), spare reins and a spare stirrup and leather, a small medical kit, a hoof pick and a headcollar. What you take where depends on you, your horse's needs, and the equipment you have to choose from. It may be impossible for you to carry more than just a few items to the Steeplechase, because of its location. Just stuff a few studs into your pocket, grab a rein and an Easy Boot, and go! These are just suggestions for you to use or disregard as you see fit.

So there you have it. Work from a well-organised and efficient base and the Events should come easily to you. Your job will become a routine, and your gift for being able to get under the skin of all your horses (ask yourself: 'Is this going to help the horse or hinder him?') will ensure that all the horses are fit and cared for in the best possible way.

CHAPTER THREE

Travelling

Travelling is an inescapable part of Eventing life. For the groom, it is one of the biggest responsibilities: getting the horses from place to place safely and on time. Travelling can be a great deal of fun and it is one of the factors that most attracts grooms to join the ranks of the Eventing world.

All journeys with horses, whether long or short, should be well planned and well thought out to cover all eventualities, however small. Making sure you get enough sleep before any journey seems an obvious point to mention, but it is worth remembering when you realise that most trips entail early starts and long drives. Even though you are sitting down and are ostensibly fairly inactive, driving is tiring – especially when you have the additional worry of caring for the horses. Then, when you arrive, there is the unpacking and the horses to take care of. Organise everything well in advance and have everything packed and ready to go in good time, so that you will have a clear mind and only the job in hand to worry about.

Most of the travelling that you do will be in your own country and therefore restricted to motor vehicles. But for the lucky ones there is the chance of travelling by sea and air to international events. Basically, the preparations are the same for all, with just the extra procedures and papers to know about for international travelling. Quarantine regulations vary considerably around the world and some are severe enough to necessitate a horse spending several weeks – or even months – in a restricted area. So do find out, well in advance, what the quarantine procedure will entail. We will try to cover, step by step, the things that a groom should know and do when preparing horses for travel and for when you are with them on the journey.

Travelling by road

The primary aim is to make sure that you have done everything you can at home in order to make the trip successful. Whether you have a van or a truck and trailer, keeping them in good repair and regularly serviced should be the first consideration. Make it your business to learn basic mechanics, such as checking the oil, the water, and the tyre pressures. Know how to change a tyre and make sure that you have the tools for the job. Keep in the vehicle all the necessary papers that you may need in an emergency, such as insurance and registration documents; also any insurance papers relating to the horses.

Before leaving you will of course know that accommodation has been arranged both for you and the horses. Keep up-to-date maps with you. You should also have a small diary in which to record the routes to each Event, the time it takes, and any notes about the journey that may be of help for the following season.

Make sure that the interior of the horse van or trailer is safe for your horses. Check that the floorboards are sound and that the ramps are safe and will withstand the passage of the horses up and down. Measure the height and width of the vehicle and know roughly how much it weighs. Have this information readily available somewhere inside the cab, so you will always know if the vehicle can fit through or over any bridge, tunnel or narrow space.

Have with you at all times a small first-aid kit for humans, as well as one for the horses. Always keep a good supply of loose change and enough money with you to get you out of any trouble. Do not forget to take with

Travelling equipment for the horse, neatly arranged outside the stable, ready for loading into the van or trailer.

you the Omnibus Schedule, so that you have details of how to get to the Events.

Should you be using commercial transport, pick a reputable organisation rather than trying to save money, which is a false economy. A good professional outfit, chosen through personal recommendations, is far more likely to provide experienced and careful employees than a backroad set-up, where the equipment may be faulty or old and knowledge of insurance and animal handling may be non-existent. Make sure that they thoroughly clean the interior of their horse box with disinfectant, so that your horses do not pick up any germs from the previous occupants. If you meet resistance with this request they are not as efficient as they should be. Anyway, it is a good idea to carry with you a spray gun of disinfectant just in case.

Equipment
If you are planning a trip that will take you away from home for a week or more, and one that will include a Three-Day Event, then the packing of all the equipment is a gigantic task: one that has to be thought out well ahead of time and planned down to the last detail. Even the most well-seasoned groom will tell you that lists are a necessity and are what planning is really all about. Good planning will ensure that you are as close to one hundred

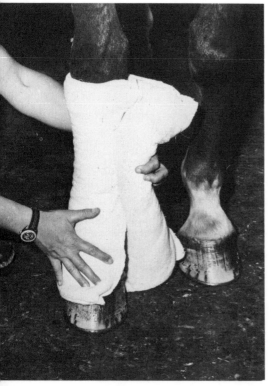

Travelling bandage.
(A) The under-padding is thicker than for a stable bandage, to give maximum protection while the horse is in transit. The inner and outer edge of the padding must start and end on the cannon bone, never on the tendons.
(B) The bandage must stretch well over the coronet band and bulbs of the heel, touching the ends of the shoe.
(C) The bandage is secured at the top, on the outside of the leg.

A

per cent efficiency as is humanly possible. If you have done your work at home methodically, there should be no need for the last-minute rush to the tack store to collect repairs or to buy new tack. This all leads to panic and wasted time, which you can well do without.

Sit down and go through, one by one, the jobs that you will be doing while you are away. Make a list of the tools and equipment that you will need. Start with mucking out, feeding, grooming, etc. Have two lists for the horses – one for tack and the other for items such as blankets and other individual belongings. Make a list, also, of miscellaneous objects such as blacksmith's tools, extra hooks and nails, mirrors and flashlights. Finally comes the list of things for yourself: the clothes that you take being of major importance. You must be sensibly equipped for all kinds of weather.

When you are planning a foreign trip, do a little research. Find out if you know anyone who has been to that particular Event before, and pick their brains. If, for example, it is a hot climate and there is a severe bug and fly problem, they will probably be able to advise you on some useful items to pack and will give you a general idea of what to expect.

Once all your lists are made, read through them and see what packing space you have, what you have to buy and what you really do not need. For your own peace of mind it would help to be able to take every item in the yard. But it is usually the groom – very often single-handed – who will have

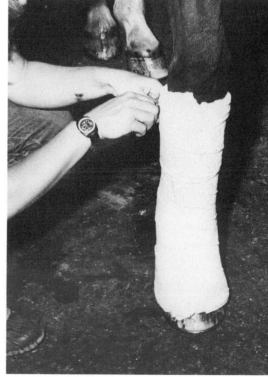

B   C

to load and unload all the equipment. So, bear this in mind when you pile twenty pounds of extra lead into one of the trunks!

If you have a tail-board on which you intend to pack luggage, try to use it only for the trunks and not for the feed or hay. If there is no alternative, wrap the hay and feed in polythene, so that the exhaust fumes will not taint and ruin them.

Pack everything methodically so that anything you may need on the journey will be readily accessible. Items such as extra blankets, medicine chest and bridles should be packed last, in case you have to unload on to the side of the road because of a mechanical failure.

How you equip your horses will depend on the weather, the length of the journey, and how well they travel. Use headcollars that are well fitting, that will not rub and, preferably, that are sheepskin-covered. The legs should be wrapped from the hocks and knees down to the coronet band, and it is even worth considering the use of bell boots for further protection of the heels and coronet band, especially when transporting horses by air

Loading should be carried out quietly and safely. Here a helper is encouraging the horse up the ramp. Note the long, thick bandages and the tail bandage; also the half-opened windows for ventilation.

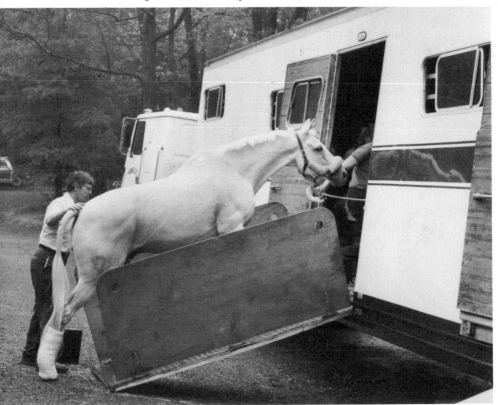

or sea, when they may panic. The snag about using bell boots is that because they are made of rubber they cause the feet to sweat, so put them on just before they are likely to be needed, such as just before loading, taking off, or on a particularly rough journey.

A poll guard, which is a padded head guard usually made of felt and leather, may also be used. This attaches to the halter and over the ears and prevents the horse from hurting himself should he go up and bang his head.

A tail bandage will protect the tail from rubbing. However, on long journeys it may slip, and if you tie it too tightly it will cause damage and discomfort. Tail guards are preferable; they do the same job as tail bandages but have two advantages – firstly, they do not have to be put on tightly and, secondly, they attach to the surcingle, so they will not slip down. Knee pads and hock boots are items used extensively in England but not so much in the United States. They are pads made of leather and felt, or high-density foam that protect the knees and hocks from bangs and scrapes.

The main thing to remember about all the gear you may put on your horse for travelling is that it must be checked during transit, not only to make sure it has not slipped but also to see that it is not doing any damage. If a bandage is too tight, it can cause damage to the tendons; if too loose, it may slip down and be rendered useless, or become twisted and cause a pressure point on the tendon. This can also happen very easily with hock and knee pads. So on long trips strip off all the wraps and other clothing, hand-rub the legs, and then re-apply the protective gear.

Even if your van or trailer has slip-proof rubber mats, always try to put down some kind of bedding – either straw or shavings – so that your horse feels comfortable enough to stale (urinate) whenever he needs to. Some horses when travelling in a horse box will not stale, however great the urge; so on a long trip it really is worthwhile to stop somewhere along the route so that he can be unloaded and allowed to relieve himself.

Pack all the equipment that you can in the van during the evening before you leave, so that in the morning all that you have to load is the horse.

Now a final recap. The trailer or van is packed, your horses are dressed appropriately, and you have all the papers, money and maps you will need for the trip. Allow for extra time 'just in case something happens', and off you go. Checking the horses during the journey is a must, although the frequency of the checks depends on how well the horses travel and what the weather is like. For instance, if it is very hot, it is advisable to stop every hour to give them water. Check that they are happy and that the trip is not distressing them. If it is, perhaps driving more slowly would help. Make sure that they are neither too hot nor too cold, that they have enough hay to munch on during the trip, and that their halter is not coming untied or beginning to rub them. On long journeys, it really is worth the time and trouble to re-do the leg bandages, as mentioned above. It is also worth remembering that in cold weather it is preferable to put more rugs on your horse, rather than closing up all sources of fresh air.

One last point to remember – always take a bucket and water with you, even on short journeys. Some horses take a while to get used to strange water and if you pick some up on your trip it might upset the horse and put him off drinking altogether. So take enough water to quench the thirst of all your horses. Just having it available will bring you peace of mind – and the horses will certainly appreciate it.

The next thing to consider is your plan of action once you arrive at your journey's end, which will be covered in more detail further on in the Eventing section of the book. Meanwhile here are a few pointers that apply to any journey. If it has been a long trip and the horse has been a little 'up-tight' throughout because of nerves or inexperience, then he needs to walk around for a few minutes to loosen up his muscles and generally to relax. (This is also important on your way back from an Event, when you will be hauling a horse that is already very tired and more than a little stiff.) So on arrival always hand-walk the horse until he has relaxed, cooled-off (if the trip has made him hot), and has been given time to urinate. Allowing the horse to graze for a few minutes will help to relax him, but make sure that it is an unrestricted area and that it is safe. If there is a chance that the grass has been sprayed with chemicals you should not allow your horse to eat until you have found out for certain that it is safe for him to do so. Also, keep the horse away from any plants that you do not recognise.

Put him in the stable and let him roll if he wants to. This is excellent mental therapy for the animal, even if he is grey and therefore difficult to keep clean. Better a dirty, but happy, horse than a clean and unhappy one. Again, depending on the length of the journey, your own schedule, and the horse's attitude, a little hay after he has been offered a drink is probably all he will need for an hour or so, until he is relaxed enough to be offered a feed. In new surroundings there are so many things for the horse to investigate that he has little time to eat. So to prevent him from being overfaced by feed all the time, wait until you think he will happily eat something before you offer it to him.

Another precautionary measure which many people take when they are away from home is keeping the horse in thick protective stable or standing bandages to prevent damage to the legs when rolling in a strange stable.

Feeding
Obviously, if you are travelling and competing on the same day, or if the trip is not a mammoth expedition, there is no need to change the horse's regular rations. On longer journeys, where he will be doing nothing but playing passenger, you must consider his feed carefully. A cut in his protein intake – and this means oats, high protein pellets and maize – is desirable if you want to avoid problems with a sick or stocked-up horse. When there is a chance that the journey will be particularly gruelling – for instance, if you are flying – cutting down the feed should start a couple of days before the departure date. Give him a good mash as the last feed before setting out; this will be easy on his stomach and will to some extent prevent stocking-up. As far as possible, try to keep to the horse's normal feed times on the journey. See if you can fix up some type of feed manger for him and take pre-packed individual feeds in separate bags. This will make life

easier, as you will not have to scramble through all the luggage to find the feed sacks.

Always have hay available for the horse to chew on – it will help to keep him occupied and out of any mischief that might be caused by boredom. The only time when it is really not worth feeding hay on a trip is when you are driving to a One-Day Event. On these competition days your horse will be galloping, so the less hay he has on the morning before the Event, the better his wind will be.

On trips taking several days such as crossing the States, you should consider having the vet 'oil' the horse. This entails drenching him with mineral oil as a preventive measure against impacted colic – something that a horse is prone to when standing on a van for days on end, munching hay and maybe deprived of his full water intake.

Travelling by air

Flying with horses is exciting, and it is something that few grooms will experience. It certainly is an experience, for you are able to see behind the scenes, both at the airport and at the quarantine station. The biggest problem that you will have is trying to stay awake through it all!

Flying horses anywhere is a long drawn out business, with a great deal of waiting about – most of the time for officials to check you, the horses, and the luggage. While all the turmoil is going on, the groom must be totally alert to the fact that she is there to look after the horses. And remember that for the horses this will probably *not* be the best experience of their lives – with all the noise and fumes and a variety of people appearing at all hours to poke, prod and check. In fact, all in all it is the furthest thing from a horse's normal daily routine that you can possibly imagine. It is up to you to help by being alert and prepared for anything. So before you rush out on wild pre-departure shopping sprees, think more about having a few early nights. And take a large flask of coffee with you on the journey.

Transporting horses from one country to another entails a great deal of paper work, and may involve a stay in quarantine. All horses must have passports as well as – depending on your country of origin and your destination – many other documents related to health and well-being. However, all of this will be taken care of either by the Team Manager, if you are travelling as part of a Team, or by the bloodstock agency through whom most travel arrangements are made. Nevertheless it will be up to you to make sure, in advance, that you have played your part by arranging for the vet to take blood samples for all the necessary tests that are required by the host country. All this information can be, and should be, obtained early from your bloodstock agency or Team Manager. If you do not know, ASK!

Equipment
Usually luggage is restricted, so packing has to be well thought out. Generally when you travel as part of a Team the Team Manager will bring along a lot of communal equipment. You should therefore make a point of finding out what they will be bringing so that you will know what to leave

at home. Make sure that you have everything marked and that you keep a list of everything you take. Use a sturdy trunk and lock it but make sure that you have a key and that a duplicate is with the Team Manager.

Some medicines are illegal in certain countries. Find out about these, and, best of all, let your Team Vet or Manager take care of them on the trip.

Feeding

Feeding comes under the same problem heading. For instance, when the British Team travel to the United States, they are offered all types of pellets and sweet feeds that are far higher in protein than most of the ones available in Britain. This also applies to the hay – virtually no alfalfa is fed in England and it is therefore dangerous to start feeding it because of the risk of colic or protein poisoning. It is better for the horses to live on straight oats, bran and meadow or seed hay. Feed what you and your horse both know and are happy with. It may seem dull, but it is safe – and you can always add apples and carrots.

We have already spoken of cutting the feeds down before travelling. Make sure that the last meal before the long journey is a mash. Feeds *en route* should be made up of small, easily digested meals, with bran as the bulk. Take along a good supply of carrots and apples, or anything that will entice the horse both to eat and to relax. This is especially important when you are taking off or landing. All the noise and movement may easily scare a horse, but if he has a groom beside him whom he knows and trusts, and if that groom also happens to have a bag of carrots – this can make all the difference between a smooth trip and one that might end with a scared or injured horse.

Once you have finished your packing, collected all the necessary papers, and prepared for any emergencies at home by leaving telephone numbers and addresses for your stand-in or back-up grooms, you will be ready to set off for the airport. Of course the procedures differ according to the location of your home base and your destination. However, the first thing to remember is that the journey is a long one, and it is important that you do everything you can to make the horse comfortable and relaxed.

At airports there are handlers who are trained and paid to get the horses on to the 'planes. Often it is easy to become very possessive and to resent the fact that strange men will be taking over your horse while they are loading. Be patient. Offer help and be there all the time – but let them do their job. They have probably handled hundreds of horses – the majority of them young, scatty thoroughbred racing stock, so your Event horses should be a pleasant change for them.

There are several methods of transporting horses by air: the most common and the safest being in a crate. The horses are loaded two at a time into a container that is very similar to a trailer. This is then elevated up into the aircraft and the whole crate is moved into place and strapped to the floor. There is enough room in front of the horses' heads for you to stand, and there is always a container of water and a bucket in each crate.

At this point, keeping an eye on the horse's temperature is essential if you want to prevent him from catching a chill. Before take-off the interior of a plane when it is loaded with animals is very hot, and your horse may be sweating through tension. Be prepared for this and act accordingly. As most of the equipment you have packed will be inaccessible from the time you reach the airport until you arrive at the other end, it is necessary to take some hand luggage for the horse for use in transit. A dustbin liner is a useful receptacle. Keep in this the feeds you will need, all pre-packed in separate bags. Take, also, a light, anti-sweat sheet, and a heavier sheet in case it gets cold, or in case you are flying to a colder climate and cannot easily get access to your gear.

Take a simple bridle with you. In most cases the airlines will stipulate that the horses must travel in bridles, so that you have more control if they panic. It is a good idea, and you are usually able to take them off once you are in the air; you can then just put them back on for landing. Once you are actually in the air, the horses travel smoothly. In fact, on most occasions, it is better than a journey by road.

Take a haynet, so that the horse has something to munch on; usually the bloodstock agency supply these. If there is no vet travelling in the plane – which is highly unlikely – take a comprehensive first-aid kit with you.

Loading horses on to a pallet which is then elevated to the loading door of the aircraft. The crate is then carefully rolled into the cargo hold and secured firmly to the floor.

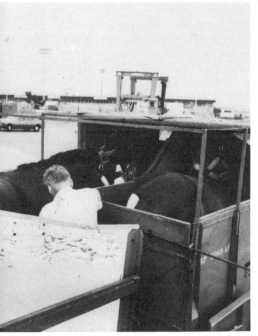

There is one sombre thought to contemplate when transporting horses by air. If a horse reacts badly to flying – begins to thrash about uncontrollably, and is a threat to the safety of the aircraft – the pilot has the authority to demand the destruction of the animal. This is a very rare occurrence – but you can see how important it is to be on the same wavelength as your horse, so that he trusts you and knows that because you are there everything is all right.

On the subject of tranquillising before flying – we think that it is unnecessary. Once you have taken off, the flight is normally very smooth, and by the time you come to land, the horses are normally accustomed to the noise and movement. If you do decide to tranquillise, ask a vet to do it. All you want is enough sedative to calm the horse. If you give him too much and he becomes a little wobbly on his legs it is possible that he may not be able to keep his balance during take-off. Once a horse has gone down in a stall on an aircraft there is very little you can do to get him up.

Though grooms must be prepared to stay with the horses for the whole duration of the flight it is not always entirely necessary. Once the horses have settled down and are munching hay quietly you may be able to snatch an hour's sleep.

At both take-off and landing it is important to be prepared for the oddest reactions from your horse. Keep hold of his head, talk to him, and bribe him with carrots if necessary. If he tries to sit down – which is the most likely thing a horse will do on landing or take-off – try to keep his head up and have someone behind hitting his rear end to keep him on his feet.

An important factor to remember when transporting horses by air is that the red tape can keep you hanging around for hours. Airport officials and handlers always seem to be having a tea or lunch break just when you need them the most. Be patient; you will not be able to hurry them and the more you hassle, the longer it will take!

Once you have arrived, the horses will have to go through a quarantine station. Depending on where you are, you may or may not be allowed to look after them through this period. Do not attempt to argue about this – the people in charge know what they are doing. Just make sure that all the gear that you send with your horse is well marked. Remove all bandages from the horse's legs before he disappears into quarantine, as they will not be checked or re-wrapped by the quarantine personnel.

The groom should wear comfortable old clothes and take a tooth-brush and toothpaste, plus a good thick book to read. Add to this a vast amount of patience and a finely tuned sense of humour, and perhaps the experience of flying with horses will be a good one and not just a memory of fighting red tape and surviving days and nights without sleep.

Travelling by sea

Today, a boat trip is a short ordeal compared with flying. There was a time when the only way to take horses abroad was to go by boat, but now this is restricted mainly to European travel. It is a simple procedure, as it entails driving your van or trailer on to a ferry and then driving it off at the other end. Much of the paper work is the same as for flying, and you will still be confronted by all those officials, checking and double-checking you and the horses. Packing is easier because you will be using your own transport and will be able to take much more equipment. Looking after the horses – their feed and the clothing they should wear – is just the same as for flying and is a matter of your own personal preference and common sense.

The advantage of going by sea is that when you arrive at the docks, you will often find that for one reason or another you have to wait. This means that you may be able to take the horses off the van to stretch their legs – and to graze if there is any grass about. But before you do this check that it is permissible. Some officials can become very irate if you unload your horse before they have cleared you through Customs – and they are quite within their rights to send you both back from whence you came for breaking the rules! Again, find out whether you can take feed stuffs into the country you are heading for. You are, at least, usually allowed to take your own hay on to the ferry, but you may be required to throw all the surplus overboard before you dock at the other end.

Before you drive on to the ferry, try to find the official in charge of loading. Explain that you have horses, and ask if it is at all possible for him to position you so that you can let the ramp down for the horses to get some air. Most officials are very helpful and will let you do this. The temperature below deck varies considerably and is quite unpredictable, so you should check that the horses are comfortable once every thirty minutes. Often when going to Events by sea you will find that you are part of a convoy. Therefore, get together with the others and work out a rota so that there is always at least one person down below and wide awake to keep an eye on the horses. This will give everyone the chance to catch up on some sleep. It is also sensible to have someone 'on duty', no matter how good the horses are, or how calm the crossing is, to prevent any unintentional outside interference. In contrast to flying, you will not have the ship to yourself. It is quite a novelty for the other passengers to see horses on a ship, and they are often keen to have a closer look. This should be tactfully discouraged, for the safety of all parties. We once found a little girl trying to feed a chicken sandwich to one of our horses.

To sum up: for a groom the actual travelling by road, sea or air is a long, tiring and often infuriating experience, fraught with seemingly pointless hold-ups. But patience is a very necessary attribute, and the importance of advance planning cannot be stressed too strongly. There are so many interesting things to see and do, but you must remember that a groom's job is to look after the horses and that this is a critical part of their preparation for an Event. They are already fit – it is your responsibility to get them from home to the Event in one piece, and happy!

CHAPTER FOUR

The Action Begins

Now the Eventing season is about to begin and the competitions are drawing nearer and nearer. You, your horse and the rider should be well prepared for the ensuing onslaught, because all the ground work has been done thoroughly, and nothing left to chance. The competitions should come as a natural progression for all of you. The first few Events of the season will be places of learning for the young and inexperienced riders, horses and grooms – and places of renewal for the old campaigners.

First of all, we have to consider two different situations when arriving at an Event. On the one hand we are talking about a One-Day Horse Trial, where you will most probably be working out of your van. On the other hand if the One-Day Horse Trial is a long way from home you may be stabling at the Event overnight. If it is a full-scale Three-Day Event you will be away for several nights.

Events where no overnight stabling is required

The night before your journey, sit down with your rider and go over all the details, especially specific tack and equipment that she or he will need. Before leaving home you will have found out the starting times by telephoning the Secretary, so you will know in advance when your horse is expected to compete. From this information you can work out when you should arrive at the show grounds, allowing time for delays and about forty-five minutes to an hour to get organised and the horses settled before they need to be ridden.

Having arrived safely at the Event, park in a place that is permissible and, if at all possible, that is strategically positioned near the Dressage and Jumping arenas. It should also afford enough shade for the horses when it is hot. While your rider goes to pick up the numbers and find out where everything is, it is your job to take care of the horses. If it has been a particularly long trip – and if there is time – take them for a hand walk to stretch their legs and allow them to have a look round. It will also give them the opportunity to urinate, which is most important. Give them all some water, and then organise your equipment.

If the weather looks as though it will stay fine, then you can set up outside. However, if it is wet, life for the groom can be particularly tiresome, as you will have to work out of the back of the van. Here it is important to be very well organised and know where everything is. Space is at a premium on these occasions, and you will have to take everything you need and keep it in a place that is easily accessible, while at the same time allowing enough space for the horses, and room to work in. You will not only have to decide how you are going to arrange all the equipment,

On arrival at an Event the groom takes the horse for a hand walk and a graze.

but also how to cope with one, two, three or more horses in a small space – sometimes in bad weather, with each horse going out at least three times.

Find out from your rider where all the arenas are located and his schedule for the day. Keep a time schedule on you all day, so there is no chance of not having a horse ready at the right time.

An Event can also be a big social occasion. It may have been months since you last saw some of the riders and grooms, but remember that there will be time enough at the end of the day to catch up on all the gossip. So if you should find yourself with nothing to do – rather than socialising, be thinking ahead. You could, for example, get the washing-down water ready, or sweep out the van. There is always something to be done and it is usually something that can make your life easier in the long run and make your whole outfit look more professional.

It is a good idea, if possible, to take your own water with you to a One-Day Horse Trial, as horses can be incredibly fussy drinkers. If you are unable to do this, try to use water directly out of a tap and avoid using ponds or troughs where other horses may have drunk; they may well have left some germs behind them! Do not tie your horse up to the van, unless you are absolutely sure that he will stand there peacefully, come hell or high water. There are so many things to frighten your horse – things that he would not normally see at home – that it is just not worth the risk of his panicking and breaking loose. Anyway there are usually at least a handful of willing helpers around who will gladly hold on to your horse while you change a saddle – so take advantage of their help.

When you are at a Horse Trial that is being held on one day only, and you are having to work out of your horse box, economical and efficient use of space is vital to make your life easier. Therefore when you are packing, plan it logically, so that you pack last of all the items that you will immediately be needing when you arrive at the other end. This means, for instance, that the tack should be packed last so that it is readily available without an embarrassing ten-minute search under blankets and haynets, which will only fray everyone's nerves.

Your first job will be to get the horse ready for the Dressage test. If you had time before you left home, you may have done the plaiting and thorough grooming there; if there is enough time once you have arrived at the Event, you can do it on the grounds. The Dressage phase of any Event is the time when appearance matters the most.

Another consideration for the Dressage phase is studs. If the arena is on grass, the rider may want some extra traction, so be prepared to put studs in at this early stage. In a sand arena, studs are generally unnecessary, as the footing is usually too deep for a stud to get any purchase and therefore to be in any way effective.

Make sure that you are familiar with the rules: that your rider is correctly dressed, that he is not carrying a whip, that he is wearing spurs (if these are compulsory for the test he is riding) and whatever other rules apply in any given situation. Again, check that you also know the rules that apply to your horse. If he wears boots to warm-up in, take them off before he enters the arena. Check that he has the correct bit, etc. If you are not sure, ask!

Horse Trials that run on one day only do not have to follow the Dressage/Cross-Country/Show Jumping order. In fact for various reasons, many organisers hold the Cross-Country last. For the groom this is by far the easiest arrangement, as it means that you are not battling against time to cool out and then re-present a well turned-out animal for the Show Jumping. Times are often tight and if your rider has two or more horses competing, your day will consist of non-stop action from beginning to end. In fact we often feel that the compensation for the Events early in the season, when you are run off your feet, comes with the relative luxury of a Three-Day Event – where you have just one, or perhaps two, horses, where time is plentiful, and a whole day is devoted to each phase.

Dealing with three horses at a One-Day Horse Trial is a common occurrence for a groom. It means nine separate competitions – each horse having to complete three phases. The groom's job will involve braiding three horses – perhaps up to ninety individual braids! You will most probably have to tack up at least nine times; perhaps even be unlucky enough to have nine different bridles, too! Then you will have to wash each horse at least twice . . . and so it goes on.

So you can see why it is important to use the early Events for gaining experience. The more Events you attend, the easier they will become and the more efficient you will be. By the time you arrive at your first Three-Day Event you should be well-seasoned and confident.

After the Dressage you will prepare the horse for either the Cross-Country or the Show (Stadium) Jumping. Depending on the level at which your rider is competing, he may have to carry a minimum weight, which may mean carrying extra lead. Find out what applies, and have all the pads and lead that you will need.

An average cross-country course for a One-Day Horse Trial takes from five to seven minutes to ride. It is your job to be at the Start, to put up the practice fences and help with the horse's warm-up, in case the rider needs any last-minute assistance. It is even more important for you to be at the Finish, with a headcollar and some sort of horse clothing – probably a string vest or warmer rugs, depending on the weather. At this point all your organisation and planning will pay off.

The first thing you must do is to check for injuries. Make sure that the horse is not overstressed and check that he still has all his shoes on. Loosen his tack, and if the weather is very hot throw some water over his throat, legs, and *in between* his hind legs, to help cool him out; do not allow cold water to splash on the hind quarters where all the big muscles are, in case this causes the horse to tie-up or get muscle cramps. Keep him walking until he has sufficiently recovered and has stopped blowing, then wash him down thoroughly and check more carefully for injuries. Any water, hay or feed offered after the Cross-Country should be given gradually, and only when the horse has recovered. If you have ninety minutes or more before the Show Jumping, try to give him a small lunch, so that he is on schedule and has something in his stomach.

Remember to use a dry saddle pad for each phase, and to wipe the tack off quickly with a soapy sponge.

65

For the Show Jumping you will have to help your rider warm up. This part of any Event is a test of the groom's courage, as it sometimes takes nerves of steel to stand next to the practice jumps – there are inevitably only two such fences for about 150 competitors and they all seem to want to jump at exactly the same time!

After the competition is finished, with any luck your rider will be off collecting his or her prize. You are still very much at work, for it is in the horse's best interests to be taken good care of after working so hard all day. Untack him and wash him if necessary. This is no problem when it is warm, but in cold weather you must make sure that your horse is never in danger of catching a chill. Try to carry hot water in such conditions, and stand the horse in a windless place. Wash off only the parts that really need it, and as quickly as you can, then towel-dry and rug up quickly.

Give him water and feed, or hay, and wrap his legs in whatever type of poultice or brace you use. While the horses are eating, pack away all your equipment. If you have been able to work methodically throughout the day, you will have put things away as you went along. If you had any quiet moments at all, you should have cleaned at least some of the tack; there is nothing worse than arriving home late at night, tired and hungry, and having to unpack a van-load of disorganised equipment and dirty tack. So keep this in mind and resist the temptation of a good gossip in between phases, even though it may seem preferable to wiping over a bridle or rolling up bandages!

One of the most important factors when you are working out of your van at Events is the weather and the way in which it affects your horses. In England in the spring the weather is so changeable that it is easy for a horse to catch a chill if the groom does not pay close attention to his temperature. Always be aware of this, especially when you are washing a horse down. Find the spot most protected from the cold winds. Or when the temperature is up in the nineties, a shady spot. Remember that a small set-back like a chill can ruin your chances of going further. Bear in mind, also, that a tired horse is a physically vulnerable horse. Be particularly careful on the journey home, and if it is a long trip, stop once in a while to check the ventilation in the horse box.

Events where you will be stabling overnight

In England, because of its comparatively small size, staying away from home is something you will usually only do when competing in a Three-Day Event. In the United States it is something that you will have to do for perhaps three out of every four Horse Trials.

At most Three-Day Events your first taste of officialdom will be the inspection of your papers. At international competitions your horse's passport will be collected, and all documents referring to immunisation shots and required blood tests should be there and up-to-date. Also, a vet will check that the horse is indeed the one you claim he is, and that he is basically fit and healthy enough to compete. This check may happen on arrival or on the following day; but be prepared for it, and have everything ready.

Your immediate task is to find out where you will be stabled. Whether you are in temporary or permanent stalls, always give them a thorough checking over before installing the horse. The following are some basic points:

1 Clean out all old bedding. You never know if the previous occupant was healthy or not. For the same reason, thoroughly clean out any feed mangers which should be disinfected, even if you do not intend to use them; horses are too curious to leave them uninvestigated and unlicked!
2 If there is an automatic water-drinker you may prefer to turn this off and use a water bucket. You can then keep an accurate check on how much water your horse is, or is not, drinking; a nuisance perhaps, but valuable information.
3 Make sure that all light fixtures are in good working condition and out of reach.
4 If the floor has a surface other than dirt – i.e. brick or concrete – check that the drain cover is intact and that there is no risk of the horse trapping his foot in it.

Many Events supply temporary stabling as shown here, and extra caution must be taken in these strange and often cramped and congested surroundings.

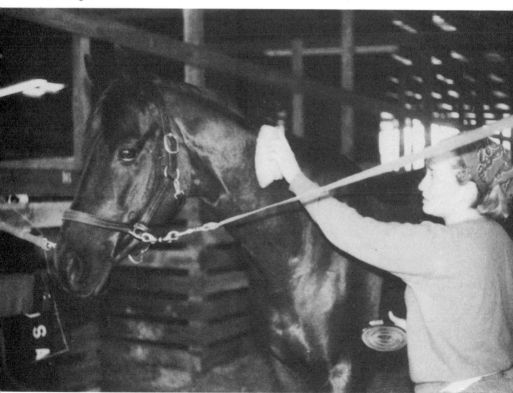

5 Check that all glass windows are out of reach of heads or heels. If in doubt, ask the stable manager to nail something up to prevent any accidents.

6 Check that there are no sharp edges or nails protruding anywhere that may cut your horse or poke an eye out.

7 Make sure that the door is strong and that the latches and bolts all work.

8 If you are ever stabled in an old yard, make sure that any pretty and seemingly innocuous ivy is out of reach of a hungry and nosy Event horse. We have seen an Advanced horse almost throw away his chance of competing because he was able to reach the ivy that adorned his picturesque stable yard; his whole mouth was swollen and extremely painful within minutes.

9 If your horse is a stallion, he will require separate stabling out of reach of other fellow competitors; this, of course, should be arranged with the organisers well before the Event.

With temporary stalls, many of the points mentioned above have to be taken into consideration, plus a few others, such as:

1 Have the stalls been put up strongly enough to keep your horse safely inside?

2 Is he likely to put a foot through the boards?

3 Before you put the bedding down, be sure to check that there are no poisonous plants growing up through the stall. A horse knows that there is a free meal to be had under bedding and we guarantee that, by morning, he will have scraped all the bedding back and eaten any grass there is.

4 Taking along some sort of anti-chewing paint is often a good idea, as horses seem to regard the wood of these temporary stalls as quite a delicacy.

5 Should you find that the partitions are low enough for your horse to have contact with his neighbours, keep a watchful eye to ensure that it does not turn into a fight. If it does, ask to be moved, or ask for an extra board to be put up.

Most of the problems can usually be rectified by having a few words with the over-worked stable manager.

When you are stabling in temporary stalls the weather will be a big consideration. Normally you will need to take extra blankets, not only because the horses will feel colder than usual, but also because there is often a dampness problem caused by condensation from the canvas or plastic roofing materials. So, again, be prepared and throw in some extra rugs, plus all the rain sheets you have; if you do not need them on the horses, if it rains you can use them over the feed and hay or over the tack trunks. Using New Zealand rugs at night is something that we have found helpful in keeping the horses warm and dry, as well as the good rugs dry and clean.

Another obvious point is not to wash a horse down in his temporary stall, unless he enjoys living in a bog! If the weather is too bad for you to wash him outside, try to find a stall that is vacant and see if you can persuade the organisers into letting you use it.

Once you have arrived and checked everything, and the horse has been walked, watered and made comfortable, it is now time to get organised. First of all, if you are hoping to use your horse box as a tackroom, find out where you are allowed to park it. Obviously this plan is useless if you have to park ten miles away; in which case you will either have to use a spare stable or to neatly arrange all your equipment around your stall area. Any equipment you will not need immediately can be kept in the horse box.

As we have mentioned earlier, it is far better to take your own feed stuffs and hay with you whenever possible. This is usually only difficult when you are travelling abroad or if you do not have the space. The more you can keep your horse to a routine that he is used to – and this includes feed times, work times, grazing, and feed stuffs – the happier he will be; which, in turn, means that your life will be that much easier.

After you have found your tackroom and have unloaded all your gear, note where the light switches are before it gets dark. One groom we know

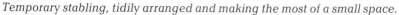

Temporary stabling, tidily arranged and making the most of a small space.

needed lights for the first time in a strange stable in order to braid for an early Dressage. As she had not the slightest idea where the switches were there followed an hour's unnecessary panic . . . and twenty rotten braids!

Before you leave the stable area, write out clearly on a card the horse's name, the rider's name, the rider's telephone number, your telephone number, and your room number if you are in an hotel. If you are on the grounds, state where your tent or caravan is located, just in case of an emergency.

Another important point to check is where to obtain feed and bedding. At most Events there are set times when you can order these items, so find out the times and try to make the workers' lives a little easier by not turning up at ten thirty at night to demand some oats for 'Dandy' because you have only just discovered that you are out of them.

Ask where you may clip, should you want to. There is usually a stall that has an electric outlet. Check that you have all the correct plugs and adaptors.

Most of the information you need can be obtained from the stable manager who, in every case in our experience, is worth his weight in gold. They seem to be able to do the impossible, such as keep fifty odd grooms, riders and horses happy, on practically no sleep and a diet of constant, 'Do you have an extra stall?', or 'Can you pull my car out of the mud?' and other time-consuming problems. It is from the stable manager, or the notice board outside his office, that you and your rider will obtain all the information you need to know, such as starting times, where you are allowed to ride, and when feed, etc., will arrive. Also, you can usually get in touch with the blacksmith or the vet through the stable manager. Always bear in mind that he is busy and that the less you disturb him, the better it will be; however, he is always glad to help you when you really need it. If you do have to ask him anything, be sure to pass on any useful information to your fellow competitors as it will benefit them and will also save the stable manager from answering the same question fifty times over. Of course, if you are grooming as part of an international team, any questions you have should be directed to your Team Manager or the Chef d'Equipe.

Even if your horse does not normally get a late-night feed, it really is advisable to make a habit of checking him later on each night, just to make sure everything is all right. It is even more important to check that he is warm enough. You never know how different stables contain or let out the heat until you see for yourself. So, for your horse's good and your own peace of mind a late-night check is strongly advised.

While we are on the subject of late-night feeding, try to get together with your immediate neighbours and compromise over a feed time, so that the horses do not get disturbed ten times in a night; perhaps this may even work in the mornings.

On the evening of arrival you should take the horse's temperature, and check it daily thereafter.

Before you retire for the night, collect your groom's pass and try not to lose it! As a rule they are sent to the riders or given out on arrival; usually

A neatly turned-out groom hacking a well-groomed horse, which is wearing an exercise rug. Note the long rein required under the rules.

they are not needed but at the bigger Three-Day Events they are vital if you want to be able to move around freely.

Always be aware of the overall appearance of your stable area. Does it look clean and tidy? Does it reflect a conscientious groom and outfit? It should do. If you make a habit of putting everything back in its place after you have used it, not only will the place look tidier but you will also be able to find the tools more quickly if they are where they should be. Remember, it is an indication of how much you care and how efficient you are. So keep things as you would at home.

The groom cleans out and repacks the stud holes to ensure the studs will screw in easily once the competition begins.

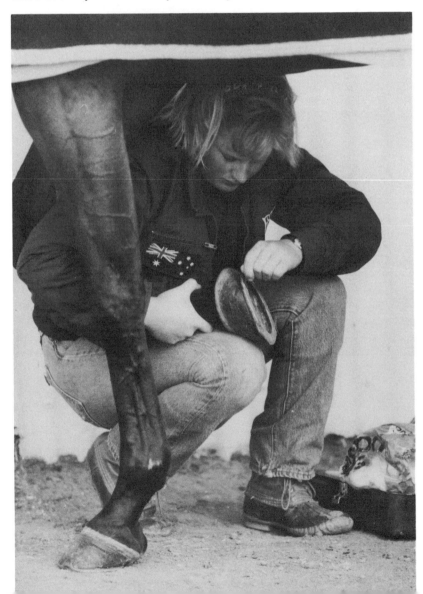

CHAPTER FIVE

Tests, Trials and Events

In England the term Horse Trials covers every type of Eventing, from the Combined Test that only has two phases to the Three-Day Event which is the aim and ultimate goal of every Event rider. In the United States, Eventing, or Combined Training, describes the sport in general. In both countries, specific titles are used to differentiate between competitions which offer a full-scale Speed and Endurance Test and those with a considerably modified version. For the sake of clarity, in this book we are using the following definitions:

Combined Tests Consist of two phases only – a Dressage test, followed by a Show Jumping test.

Horse Trials Consist of three phases – Dressage, Cross-Country, and Show Jumping. The Dressage test is always first; after that, the order of the remaining two tests may vary. Sometimes, and particularly in the United States, a Horse Trial may be held over two or even three days.

Hunter Trials A Hunter Trial, not to be confused with a Horse Trial, is often run by the local Hunt and is usually a cross-country competition, won by either the fastest time, or the competitor closest to a previously set 'optimum time'. Sometimes a show jumping competition is run concurrently, but it does not count towards the outcome of the Hunter Trials. These are excellent learning places for young horses, riders and grooms.

Two-Day Events   A modified version of the Three-Day Event, where the Show Jumping follows the Dressage test on the first day. The Speed and Endurance is held on the second (final) day and, in some cases, Phase A – the First Roads and Tracks – is omitted entirely. It has the advantage of giving horses and riders the experience of the various phases of the Speed and Endurance Test without over-emphasising the stress factor. Sometimes, because of the number of entries, a Two-Day Event is held over three days!

Three-Day Events   Consist of three separate tests, each run on separate days, but with four different phases on Cross-Country day. The Dressage is held first, followed the next day by the Speed and Endurance Test, which has four distinct phases – A and C, which are Roads and Tracks; B, which is Steeplechase; and D, which is the Cross-Country. The Show Jumping is held on the final day. Many people feel that the term Three-Day Event is a misnomer as the competition may be held over four, or even five days. However, the term is intended to describe the type of competition and should not be taken absolutely literally.

Thinking about Eventing conjours up visions of Three-Day Events, with their tough, gruelling courses, the crowds and the excitement and tension that increases as the days creep on towards the Sunday and the final Show Jumping test. Unfortunately for the spectator, but mercifully for the horse perhaps, most of the Eventing season consists of One-Day Horse Trials and Combined Tests. There may be a few Two-Day Events along the way but generally the Three-Day Event is at the end of the season. This is the culmination and final proving ground of all the work that you, the horse and the rider have put into the preceding three months. There are usually only one or two major national Three-Day Events in each season, but for the lucky few there are also the foreign Events. The gradual run-up from Horse Trials and Combined Tests to Three-Day Events is logical for many reasons. First of all, working on the principle that you must 'learn to walk before you can run', it is only fair to the horse that there should be a step by step advance towards such a demanding competition as a Three-Day Event. Also, there are a great many people who do not make it to the top in Eventing, or who do not even want to; quite a number of competitors derive enormous pleasure from simply riding at Horse Trials and never even contemplate a Three-Day Event.

Horse Trials are competitions but they are also valuable learning grounds – not only for the horse and rider, but also for the groom. As they are run along different lines from a Three-Day Event, a groom should know what to expect, and in this chapter we will try to explain, in greater detail, all the different types of competition you are likely to come across, and what each competition offers to the Event rider, horse, and groom.

Eventing is essentially the combination of two or three disciplines – Dressage, Cross-Country, and Show Jumping. There are also different levels of competition to accommodate everyone, according to ability and/or experience. A One-Day Horse Trial may offer a Novice class and an

Intermediate class, as well as an Advanced class, depending on the demand and on the organiser's facilities. In the United States, it would be rare for more than two different levels to be offered at a One-Day Horse Trial.

Combined Tests

The first step on the ladder is the Combined Test, comprising two of the disciplines – Dressage and Show Jumping. These competitions offer a rider the chance to enter a horse that is not necessarily fit enough to tackle a cross-country course. It also affords a perfect opportunity to take young horses for their first taste of competition. Many people make use of Combined Tests to practice their Dressage and Show Jumping in a competition atmosphere, without actually tiring the horse with an endurance phase; this enables riders to compete at Combined Tests as often as they like, without affecting the horse's fitness programme. For example, a rider could compete at a Combined Test on a Thursday without jeopardising the horse's health and well-being when he competes at a Horse Trial on the following Saturday. So you can see how valuable these competitions are, how useful they can be in the training and education of young horses, and how they can be used as a rehearsal for older horses, or

This horse is being grazed at the edge of a practice arena to accustom him to all the activity while he is still relaxed. Note the warm rug and protective polo bandages.

just as a break in routine. Sometimes the older, well-seasoned horses start to become bored, and an outing to a Combined Test is just what they need to keep them happy.

For the groom, a Combined Test provides an excellent opportunity to practice your turning-out skills. Just because a Combined Test is not a top competition, there is no excuse for being lax about turn-out. No matter what the occasion, your horse's appearance is a direct reflection of your competence. A Combined Test will also show how your horse reacts when he is away from home – particularly if he is at the start of his eventing career – and will be an indication of how he will react later on at the bigger competitions. Horses are all different. Those that seem quiet as lambs and imperturbable at home may be the most agitated and difficult to handle once they are away.

Horse Trials

A Horse Trial consists of all three disciplines, always with the Dressage first. Then come the Cross-Country and the Show Jumping – though not necessarily in that order; in fact in England most Horse Trials are run with the Cross-Country last. These are the competitions that for the groom will take up most of the season.

The day will be fairly hectic, depending on the times that your rider has been allocated. The organisers work out the timetable, and three or four days before the Trials start should notify the rider of his Dressage, Cross-Country and Show Jumping times. You will have to prepare the horse for three different phases, which entails a great deal of hard work, versatility and stamina. Should you have more than one horse, and if you want to ensure that everything will run smoothly, you will have to plan the day thoroughly and thoughtfully.

Dressage is the first phase and is normally held fairly early in the day. Then come either the Cross-Country and the Show Jumping or vice-versa. From the groom's point of view it is much easier when the Cross-Country comes last, as once this phase is over the groom can spend as much time as she likes cooling out the horse and seeing to his needs, without having to rush. When the Cross-Country happens before the Show Jumping the groom has very limited time in which to cool out the horse and have him clean and presentable for the last phase. It may seem idle to carp, but if you should ever have three or four horses at a One-Day Horse Trial with the Cross-Country in the middle, you will see how tight time can be for you, even though the organisers have done their best to sort things out. Also, if you are very rushed, the horses are in danger of being neglected. Imagine a muddy day, three or four sets of dirty tack to clean, plus a horde of steaming and muddy horses to cool out and groom in a matter of an hour or two! Of course it is not always that bad, and as you gain more experience it will seem like nothing.

Grooms should use these Trials to practice such things as putting in studs, sewing bandages, and finding out how each horse – and rider – will react in the atmosphere of a competition. The observant groom will learn

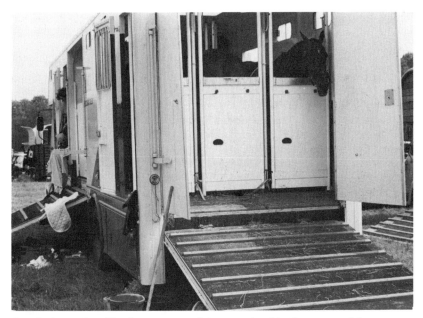

Ready for action. The horses are safely contained in the van and the equipment is about to be neatly organised outside it.

many of the rider's undiscovered quirks and requirements. Some riders, just like some horses, can be totally different at an Event from when they are at home. Even organised riders can forget the simplest thing once they are at a competition: you may find yourself constantly running after them with their hat or gloves, or reminding them of their numbers and times.

So all grooms should view even the lesser Horse Trials with respect. Expect, and be prepared for, everything and anything to happen – and always remember that the horses come first. When you arrive home with a bunch of dirty horses and tack it is easy to lose sight of the ultimate goal. But you will have learned something, and it is this constant learning that will give you the know-how and confidence to tackle the bigger challenges that await you at a Three-Day Event.

The one factor that Horse Trials and Combined Tests usually have in common is that in all probability the groom will be working out of the horse box or trailer. This calls for organisation of the highest order, as already described in the previous chapter.

Two-Day Events

The next step up from a Horse Trial is the Two-Day Event: a sort of pipe-opener for Three-Day Events in that the Speed and Endurance Test has all the same phases. The competition begins with a Dressage day, which may sometimes run over two days if there are a large number of entries. Later on during the Dressage day the Show Jumping takes place, though occasionally it is held on the morning of the second day. Either way the last part is always the Speed and Endurance Test and this is broken into four phases, exactly as for a Three-Day Event.

Phase A, Roads and Tracks, lasts for up to fifteen minutes and warms the horse up for the next phase which is B, the Steeplechase. This is a course of steeplechase fences ridden at speed, and is followed by Phase C, more Roads and Tracks, which adds to the endurance but also gives the horse and rider a chance to recover from the efforts of the Steeplechase. Phase C is timed to take about thirty minutes or more and leads to the 'Box'. Here there is a compulsory rest of ten minutes for all competitors before the final phase, D, the Cross-Country.

As already mentioned, this competition is a logical stepping stone towards the final challenge of the Three-Day Event and provides a good chance for all concerned to practice. Particularly important is the ten-minute compulsory halt, when the groom has a vital job to do. Each of the ten minutes has to be used to the maximum and you cannot afford to waste a single second. It is here that you should learn how your horse reacts to being worked on when he is hot and probably excited and when there are many strange sights for him to see. The groom must be calm, quiet and highly efficient, doing everything possible to ensure the horse's physical well-being in the most unobtrusive way. For example, it is better to learn here, rather than at a Three-Day Event, that it is virtually impossible to take the saddle off in order to wash the horse down, because he will not stand still long enough for you to put the saddle back on again!

You can now see what each type of competition is trying to achieve and what each combination of rider and horse is hoping to prove. First of all, the Combined Test is purely a test of the horse's and the rider's ability to perform a Dressage test accurately and to jump a course of show jumps. Horse Trials are a test of all three disciplines – one step nearer the final goal. They prove the horse and rider's versatility in performing all three phases, and demonstrate the horse's courage, as well as his ability, in jumping fixed fences at speed. Horse Trials enable both horse and rider to experience a number of different types of obstacles. But they do not make any real demands on stamina.

The Two-Day Event requires a fitter horse than the One or Two-Day Horse Trial. The horse must be able to perform a Dressage test and then to tackle a Show Jumping course – both tests of skill. He must then go on to prove that he has the stamina and courage to complete up to twelve kilometres of Roads and Tracks, divided by a Steeplechase phase and followed, finally, by the Cross-Country phase, which may be up to 6,000 metres long. Now you can see why the horse has to be that much fitter for a Two-Day Event than for a Horse Trial; also why there are fewer Two-Day Events and why they are scheduled for the latter half of the season.

Three-Day Events

Finally, we arrive at the Three-Day Event, the ultimate test for horse and rider – not only of skill but also of stamina. It is in the Three-Day Event that we find the true meaning of endurance.

When it rains at an Event it usually pours, and you will be less peeved if
you are wearing suitable gear.

The competition opens with the Dressage Test, which has a day (or days) all to itself, and is designed to show the horse's obedience, suppleness, movement and presence, and the rider's skills at performing a set test accurately with style and in sympathy with the horse. The Speed and Endurance Test also has a day to itself and is the most demanding part of the competition. The Roads and Tracks, the Steeplechase, and the Cross-Country will all be longer than those in a Two-Day Event.

Many people on their introduction to the Three-Day Event are quite often amazed that the horse has actually been working very hard before reaching the final Cross-Country phase: which for the spectator is by far the most exciting phase to watch. But the Cross-Country is not the only challenge: it will test the horse's guts and ability whereas the other phases – Steeplechase and two sections of Roads and Tracks will really emphasise the need for stamina on Phase D.

Finally comes the Show Jumping. In Horse Trials and Two-Day Events this proves that a horse can jump around a course of coloured obstacles with care, when he is in a state of well-being and eager to do his job. On the final day of a Three-Day Event, however, your horse will not be feeling as eager or as supple as he was at his last Horse Trial. He will be feeling the tiring effects of the Speed and Endurance and would most probably prefer to stay in his stable snoozing for the rest of the day. He will be stiff and perhaps a little sore after such tremendous exertions. Now is the time when your care and the rider's ability to get the most out of the horse will begin to tell. He must have the courage to go on, and the rider must have the knowledge to coax and warm him up beforehand, so that the effort of jumping is made as easy for him as possible.

The Three-Day Event, then, is surely the most demanding of all equestrian competitions. It requires a special horse – a master of three disciplines, a horse with intelligence and courage. Such a creature needs and deserves nothing but the best care and love, and that requires a very special groom.

The more clearly that you as a groom can understand all these elements of which Eventing is made up – the Combined Tests, and the Horse Trials, and the Three-Day Events – the more easily will you become a vital participant in the sport. Just as Horse Trials are an essential preparation for Three-Day Events, so the groom can grow from novice to leader of 'the team behind the team'. No one should underestimate the value of the 'stepping stones', which are the backbone of Eventing, providing a wealth of experiences for the horse, the rider, and the groom.

Do your best, watch others, and pick up different methods and ideas that may be of help to you. Do what your rider requires of you, while always keeping the horse as the first priority in your mind. From our experience we can assure you that if you can manage a Horse Trial with two or three horses easily and efficiently you will have no trouble dealing with a Three-Day Event.

(Left) It is essential that the horse is offered water frequently during the day at an Event, particularly in hot weather, to prevent dehydration.

CHAPTER SIX

The Three-Day Event: General

The Three-Day Event is the Event of the season for you, your rider and the horse. It is the stage on which rider and horse will perform in front of the crowds, and if you have done all your ground work thoroughly it will be successful.

It is easy to see why so much time and effort goes into preparing for such an Event. For your rider there may only be one chance each season to compete at such a prestigious competition, and it would be a great shame if this opportunity were wasted because of some stupid oversight or accident that could have been easily averted.

Although you can never predict the results of an Event with any accuracy – for, with other factors, luck can play a fairly large part – it is a simple matter to make sure that all possible safeguards are taken. Bad luck and good luck are blamed and credited for many of the happenings during the days of a Three-Day Event, but we are not so sure that these diagnoses are entirely accurate. True, many eventualities take place for which no explanation can be found, but there is usually a logical reason for most things. As a groom, you can help to minimise the risk of 'bad luck' by covering every aspect of your job fully, meticulously and methodically. Most of a groom's worth lies in experience, and the knowledge that you have gained at Horse Trials will help you to be fully prepared to tackle a Three-Day Event. This experience, along with a good, large dose of common sense, will help you to cope with the daily happenings without stress. Even if you have never been to a Three-Day Event before, you will be more than capable of dealing with it if your background work has been thorough and progressive. After all, there has to be a first time. In fact, at the World Championships in Kentucky in 1978, *Felday Farmer*, ridden by

Elizabeth Boone (now Purbrick) who finished 19th, was groomed by the amazingly capable sixteen year-old Alison Neaves. This was her first international competition – and her very first Three-Day Event, as previously she had groomed and competed only at Horse Trials. Not only did she do her job well and cheerfully, but she was a helpful and sensible member of the British team. So, take heart, and realise that a Three-Day Event is not as awesome as it may first appear!

With an understanding of how important all the seemingly boring and monotonous work of the preceding months has been, you will now fully appreciate everything you have learned: it will fall into place and act as the backbone of your knowledge and confidence, for confidence you will certainly need.

Before going any further, let us tackle the official structure behind the Three-Day Event – the rules, which all grooms and riders must understand.

All Events are run under certain rules, depending on the level of competition. At the national level you will find not only Advanced classes but also Intermediate and Novice (Preliminary). For these rules you must apply to the national body concerned, as each country has its own slightly different conditions. In the United States, for example, all competitors in the Show Jumping phase are required to wear protective head gear that is secured by a safety harness; this is obligatory and anyone failing to do so will be eliminated. In Great Britain, this rule does not apply; nor does it exist under FEI Rules, and one may wear a hunt cap or a helmet.

The next step up from national level is the international competition, and these Events are all run under FEI Rules. The Fédération Equestre Internationale is the appointed body that administers all international competitions from country to country, ensuring good and acceptable standards world-wide. The FEI keeps records of all horses competing at the Advanced national and international levels, and they issue the equine passports. For all horses competing at FEI Three-Day Events there must be a passport as proof of identity.

There are several different categories and levels of international competition. At the very top is the 'Official International Three-Day Event', or the CCIO. CC is a prefix you will often see. It stands for 'Concours Complet' and it indicates that the competition is a Three-Day Event and not a Horse Trial or Combined Test. A CCIO is the toughest type of competition and includes the Olympic Games, the World and European Championships, and the Pan-American Games. The fact that they are official *team* competitions is denoted by the letter 'O' but, in addition, they have individual awards.

Next in line is the straightforward 'International Three-Day Event', or CCI. This is a competition for international riders and is primarily an individual competition, although unofficial team competitions may be arranged. These include Events such as Badminton, Burghley, Chesterland and Kentucky, and the number of foreign nations that may be represented is not limited. A variation on the CCI is the CCF, where only one foreign nation may be represented (or, alternatively, a maximum of four riders from two or more foreign nations). Another variation is the CCA, where up to a maximum of four foreign nations may be represented. 'International Junior Three-Day Events', CCIJ for individuals, and CCIOJ for team competitions, have their own rules and classifications, though they are very similar to the senior competitions, with just a few modifications based on age. Juniors must be between 14 and 18 years old. The FEI also has similar competitions for Young Riders, who must be between 16 and 21 years old. In this category, a competition for individuals is called a CCIY and the team event is a CCIOY. All these different sets of rules enable riders to compete against roughly equal opposition. Not only do they ensure high standards from the very outset of a rider's Eventing career, but they also carry on the 'step-by-step' theme that helps everyone to progress at a sensible and logical rate.

The tougher the competition, the more rules there are, and so it is essential that riders keep their grooms informed about them. The team coach will have a set of rules for reference but all grooms should acquire a basic knowledge of the rules that apply to them. To obtain a copy of the rules, both national and international, write to your National Federation: in Great Britain the British Horse Society (BHS) and in the United States the American Horse Shows Association (AHSA).

Two rules that all grooms should be aware of at Three-Day Events are those which apply to the exercising of horses. The groom is allowed both to lunge the horse and to work it in hand but, under penalty of elimination, must never school the horse mounted in the saddle. It is permissible, of course, to ride the horse at a walk and on a long rein, and to trot from one place to another. For instance, when you are meeting your rider somewhere where he will then mount the horse, and you need to trot to get there at the appointed time, that is perfectly legal; but you are not allowed to school the horse in any way while you are on its back. Also, once you have arrived at the competition site the horse must wear his bridle numbers every time he leaves his stall, even just for a hand walk, and especially whenever he is ridden.

We will now go on to describe in a little more detail the actual schedule of happenings that are likely at a Three-Day Event. Although each Event differs slightly – in that at one the briefing may be at ten o'clock in the morning and at another at two in the afternoon – you must allow for such variations.

As will be clear by now, a Three-Day Event does not necessarily run over three days. Most are held over four days, as the Dressage is often spread over two days. In addition, the briefing and the official course-walk usually take place on the day before the first Dressage day, so you could even call it a Five-Day Event!

On arrival

There is the *First Examination*. This is to establish the horse's identity and to satisfy the veterinary official that the horse is in good health; that it is not, for instance, running a temperature or developing a cold. This examination is very informal – it can either take place as you unload your horse, or later, in the stable. The veterinary official will seek you out when you arrive. At this point you will hand in the horse's passport. Make sure that this document is up-to-date and that you have a record of all current injections. If the papers are not in order the officials are quite within their rights to disbar you from the grounds or to put the horse in isolation, thus eliminating him from the Event. This is a responsibility to be shared by both the rider and the groom.

Second day

The *Briefing*, followed immediately by the *Official Course-Walk*. These usually take place in the morning. The briefing is the official welcome by the organising body of all the competitors, owners, trainers and grooms. All the riders are expected to attend, and if the groom has the time she really should be there too, as it will be a good chance to feel the atmosphere of the Event from the very beginning. It is also an excellent opportunity for the groom to establish in her mind where everything is situated. She can, for example, find out where the neutral zones are – such as the area after the

The briefing at the beginning of a Three-Day Event is intended principally for riders, but it is of great benefit if the grooms can attend, too.

Steeplechase where one is allowed to check the horse and the rider without being penalised. At this briefing the organisers will not only welcome everyone, but will also inform you of any new rules and of any rules that are peculiar to their own Event. For example, there is generally a rule about dogs – that they are banned or only allowed in the parks if they are on a lead. A knowledge of all this information will help to make the Event run smoothly for you and your rider.

There may be a description of certain obstacles that are on the Cross-Country, or an explanation of different ways an alternative fence may be jumped – all snippets of information aimed at helping everyone. The organisers will tell you where you are allowed to exercise, where riders may gallop their horses, etc. They will then ask for questions from the floor. Before the briefing breaks up, there will be a run-through of any social occasions that are to take place. Finally, all the riders will receive an envelope which will contain their numbers (should they be required to wear them for the vet's inspection), a map of the course, a programme,

A well turned-out horse being correctly presented to the panel at the First Veterinary Inspection. Either a neatly pulled or a plaited mane is acceptable.

passes, and any invitations for cocktail parties or dances.

The officials will then proceed to guide all the riders around Phase A – the First Roads and Tracks of Speed and Endurance day; then Phase B, the Steeplechase, followed by Phase C, the Second Roads and Tracks. The lunch-break usually comes at this point, and the Cross-Country course is open to be walked by anyone at any time. Most riders prefer to walk the course for the first time on their own; this allows them to have some idea of what their horses will see, and helps them to anticipate how their own horse will react to each fence. After a rider has walked a course four or five times, he becomes so familiar with it that it is easy to forget that on Cross-Country day the horse will be seeing the fences for the first time ever!

The day before the Dressage brings the first official formality of the competition, the *First Veterinary Inspection*, at which all the competing horses are presented, in hand, to the Ground Jury, either in a drawn or alphabetical order. Each horse is led up to the Jury, who will inspect it for any injury; they will then watch it walk and trot up and down. This is to

Example of a horse being correctly jogged, or trotted up. The rider (it could be the groom) is at the horse's shoulder, and the horse is being allowed his head, giving the panel a clear view of the horse and his movement.

ensure that all horses are sound and fit enough to compete in the Event. The Jury has the power to 'spin' (the slang term for eliminate) any horse found to be lame or unfit. This is where regular jogging at home pays off (see Chapter 2, page 21). If you have practised this well you will have no problems in getting your horse to step up and trot alongside you at the inspection. Nothing looks worse than a badly jogged horse – one that either will not trot up brightly and ends up by being dragged along, or one that is over-zealous and canters sideways in front of the Panel. All this is avoidable, and is a reflection on you, your rider, and your professionalism, or lack of it. It is also time-wasting for the Panel, who will have enough horses to watch, without being obliged to wait while you repeat your circus act! Always be quiet but firm, and always trot up with a loose rein so that the Panel can see the horse is moving freely, without interference from you.

After the Inspection, the order of Dressage will be posted and you will find out your horse's number and at what time he will perform. Usually numbers may be collected then, either from the Secretary's tent or the Stable Manager's office.

Third Day: Dressage

Entries are usually so numerous that two days are needed to judge all the tests. If the Event is particularly small, then one day will accommodate all the competitors. You will have discovered your horse's number and time on the previous evening. Although it may seem that there is plenty of spare time during these two days, do not be deceived. After you have checked out the places where you will be working on Cross-Country day (i.e. the Steeplechase and the 'Box'), and have managed to find the time to walk the Cross-Country course (which you should), and have also attended to the grooming and preparation of your horse, you will find that the two days go by at a remarkable speed.

Fourth Day: Speed and Endurance

This is the most important and the most nerve-wracking day of the whole Event. All the phases on this day are governed by Optimum Times, and penalties are imposed for being over the time in any of the four phases. The speeds are determined by the level at which your rider is competing. All the following examples are for horses competing at the Advanced level, particularly in a CCIO. However, they may be changed by the Technical Delegate – should conditions such as torrential rain or a heatwave necessitate altered distances or slower speeds.

Speed and Endurance day begins with *Phase A, First Roads and Tracks*, which usually lasts for between fifteen and twenty minutes and enables the rider to warm up the horse before the Steeplechase. It is ridden at an average speed of 220 metres per minute, which means that the rider can walk and trot and perhaps have a couple of stretches at the canter. Before setting off on this phase, riders must weigh out and are usually required to saddle up in front of the steward, to ensure that the correct weight is carried. At this initial weighing the crash helmet may be worn but the horse's bridle may not be included. At the final weighing (weighing-in), the bridle may be included if the rider is having difficulty making the required minimum weight. Juniors and Young Riders are not required to carry weight.

Phase B, the Steeplechase, is a course of fences of not more than 3450 metres (approx 2½ miles) – normally it is only 2560 metres (just under 2 miles) long. It is ridden at great speed; in fact, this is the fastest that a Three-Day Event horse will be required to run and it proves his ability to jump at speed. The fastest is about 690 metres per minute.

The finish of Phase B is the automatic start of *Phase C, Second Roads and Tracks.* There is always a neutral zone at the beginning of Phase C, where the rider may have his groom check the horse and even wash it down quickly. There will often be a blacksmith at this point also. The Second Roads and Tracks phase is ridden at the same speed as the first, but the distance is greater and usually takes about forty-five minutes, enabling the horse to recover sufficiently before he reaches the Box. It is also a very important part of the endurance factor.

At the end of Phase C a panel of judges and veterinary officials check that the horse is sound and not distressed. This *Second Inspection* takes place in the Box, an area designated for the ten-minute compulsory halt, where the horses may be untacked and washed and cooled down. If the horse is not sound enough or fit enough to continue at the end of this compulsory rest, the panel may eliminate him from further competition.

Phase D, the Cross-Country, is what we all think of as the focal point of Eventing. It consists of a course of up to 7000 metres (just under 4½ miles) in length, with approximately thirty-five obstacles, to be jumped at an average speed of 570 metres per minute – a good strong gallop. At the end of Phase D the rider will weigh-in and the horse will have a second examination. When the horse has recovered sufficiently the veterinary official will give permission for him to be taken back to the stables. Should the horse be distressed, the vet can tell you to take him back in a vehicle, or he may advise some other procedure. The official cannot eliminate any competitor at this stage, but may merely advise on the best course of action for the horse's well-being; he will report any findings to the Ground Jury.

Fifth Day: Show Jumping

Before the Show Jumping phase begins there will be a *Third Veterinary Inspection.* This is held in the morning and follows the pattern of the first inspection. All horses will trot up in front of the same Ground Jury, who will have the power to eliminate any horse that is deemed lame or not fit enough to continue. This is for everyone's good, especially the horse's, as it precludes any cruelty or harm that could occur if an unfit horse were allowed to participate in the Show Jumping.

At about noon there is traditionally a parade of competitors before the actual test begins. The jumping is usually run in reverse order of placing, meaning that the horses in the lead will jump last, which adds to the excitement. The jumping competition is then followed by the prize-giving and the end of the Event. All numbers should now be handed in and Dressage score sheets collected. Passports will also be returned.

We would like to add a final note concerning the veterinary inspections and examinations. All these are for the good of the horse and therefore of the sport, as they encourage the best care for the horse. There is one main difference between an Examination and an Inspection.

An EXAMINATION is carried out by experts, among whom is a veterinary official. They do not have the power to eliminate a rider from the competition, but only advise the rider if there is cause for concern – in which case they will report their findings to the Ground Jury.

An INSPECTION, of which there are three, is a more formal affair. It is conducted by the Ground Jury, which includes a veterinary official and which has the power to eliminate any horse considered to be lame or unfit to continue.

It is important for you to understand the difference in significance of these two formalities, the Examination and the Inspection.

As you can see, a Three-Day Event is a test for all those concerned – the horse, the rider and the groom. Such a challenge needs a close-knit team, each doing a separate job but all working together efficiently towards the ultimate goal of winning.

It is a fairly easy task to list the equipment that a groom will need at a Three-Day Event. It is not too difficult to outline the situations that you should be prepared for during that hectic week. What is more difficult to describe is the emotional strain that a groom is likely to undergo. It does not matter if you are fifty and have been Eventing for twenty years – this is no guarantee that things will run according to plan. In fact, despite all the ground work that you do at home and despite the countless times that you check the tack or take your horse's temperature, certain things can still happen that will be totally unexpected or unwarranted. A shoe may come off on the Steeplechase. Your horse may not pass one of the inspections because of a stone bruise. Your rider may make a costly mistake. Or a fence may be your horse's 'Waterloo', causing his elimination or retirement. These are all things that happen with sickening regularity in Eventing, and they are pretty tough to handle philosophically. A groom does not just have to be strong enough to throw a bale of straw around; she must also be staunch enough inside to act in the most diplomatic and efficient way.

By the time you reach a Three-Day Event you will not only know how your horse will react to all the pressures, to all the surging crowds, and to all the noises, but you will also have some idea of how your rider and you yourself will react. Tears can come easily at a tense moment – and that might be just the worst moment for your horse and rider. So, a word of

Without losing track of your time schedule, catching up with old friends can be a relaxing interlude in the hectic days of an Event.

advice – be prepared for something to go wrong, and it may never happen! This also applies to your relationship with your rider. You may find that he or she is being almost impossibly fussy or short-tempered. You have to be able to handle this calmly – it is not the time for screaming matches. As well as coping with *prima donna* behaviour from your rider, you will also have to contend with your own feelings. Try to carry out your job as well as you are able. Do a lot of deep breathing and counting to ten if necessary, but stay cool. If you are properly prepared, you will be able to act promptly and correctly in any situation – whether it be changing studs at the last minute or putting on an Easyboot in record time. All these tasks require a cool, level-headed groom. An emotional heap will not help anyone.

Sadly, there are the times when the horse gets hurt. No one likes to see this happen and it can be heart-breaking for the groom, who is probably very close to the horse and obviously will be distressed. But it is a risk that exists every time a horse and rider go through the starting flags of any Cross-Country course.

CHAPTER SEVEN

The Three-Day Event: Dressage

Depending on the number of entries, there may be two days of Dressage. If this is the case, and your horse performs on the first day, then it will give you more time to prepare for Cross-Country day. Should there be only one day of Dressage tests, or should your horse be drawn to compete on the second day, you will be hard pressed and your time-table must be carefully planned.

Dressage day does not just consist of a seven- or eight-minute test. Your rider will need time to warm up, and may also plan to give the horse a pipe-opener on that day. In addition, you may need to clip the horse after his test. These are contingencies that we will cover later on in the chapter.

The Dressage arena is the ideal show place for the groom's behind-the-scenes prowess. Turnout is of paramount importance. Should you be lucky enough to be representing your country, it is not only a reflection of you and your team, but it can add or subtract valuable marks to or from the final Dressage score. Nowadays Dressage marks play a more and more decisive part in the final outcome. Throughout the world, cross-country riding has improved and levelled off, and a dashing, clear cross-country round no longer necessarily compensates for a bad or mediocre Dressage score. So your skills can have a vital influence – maybe only a matter of one or two marks, but at the end of the day they can be the difference between first and tenth place. So keep brushing!

The night before, you will have been able to study the schedule of starting times. This is printed after the First Vet's Inspection and is usually available at the stable manager's office. Post one up in your tack area, underline your horse's time, and memorise it. If there is more than one Dressage arena, find out which of them your horse is going to use. Ask your rider for the following information, and write it down:

1 The number of times he will ride the horse before the test.
2 The time he will wish to be in the saddle and ready to go before entering the arena for the test.
3 Which tack he will be using in the test, so that you can make sure it is spotlessly clean and all the metal work polished and shining.
4 Which studs are to be used. In uncertain weather conditions it is a good idea to take a pocketful of assorted studs and a wrench, just in case of any last-minute monsoons.
5 Has he collected the bridle numbers? If not, find out from the stable manager or secretary where to obtain them. Do this early on; it can be one of those easily forgotten things that can turn your day into a disaster. At some Events, the bridle numbers are printed on what seems to be a square foot of card. These can act like blinkers, and it is advisable to trim them so that they do not look unsightly and do not interfere with your horse's vision. At some Events (e.g. in England) the numbers are tied round the rider's waist with tapes, or worn as arm-bands.

In the morning, after you have fed, watered and mucked-out the stall, you can begin to prepare for the day ahead. Working back from the time of the test, calculate how long you will need to groom the horse – allowing extra time for those greys who always find the dirtiest corners to roll in the night before Dressage! Having estimated how long it will take to plait, put the studs in, and tack up; add an extra fifteen minutes for the finishing touches and for any hold-ups that may have occurred due to nerves!

There are many different and acceptable ways of plaiting or braiding. As long as the end result is neat and either emphasises a good neck or disguises a poor one, the method you use is a matter of personal preference. Make sure that the tail is smart – either well pulled or plaited. There are various ways of enhancing a horse's looks, such as by drawing checker-board squares or racing stripes on the hind quarters. These are made by applying a damp brush or comb in certain patterns against the lay of the hair to accentuate the muscle. You can wipe a little baby oil around the eyes and muzzle to add shine and depth.

Tail coats always look elegant in a Dressage arena and are usually no trouble. But, again, make sure that your horse is fully used to them. Some horses object strongly to a piece of cloth tickling them across the loins, and they show their displeasure by turning in a very unorthodox test, where bucking and squirming seem to be the order of the day. So this is something else for you and your rider to work out at home, long before the Event.

Some horses, either because of nerves or through lack of schooling along the way, have the irritating habit of grinding their teeth throughout a test or, for that matter, any time they are ridden. A remedy that can be applied as a last resort just before the test is rubbing a bar of soap, such as glycerine, along the cutting surfaces of the front and back teeth, as far as you can manage to reach without undue risk. It sounds barbaric, but it seems to work on most horses because they can no longer get any sort of purchase to make grinding possible. This also helps the rider to keep the

Lungeing is a commendable practice for warming up horses before they are ridden. The groom is allowed to do this, but care must be taken to find a quiet spot where you are not in anyone else's way.

horse softer in his mouth. It can't be too terrible – we know of more than one child who has had the same treatment for bad language!

If you are part of a team, it is advisable to sew the flag cloth (that is displayed under the saddle) to the saddle pad to prevent it from slipping. This mishap was experienced by a British team member some years ago, and it was both distracting and embarrassing, as well as downright detrimental to the quality of the test. All you need is a tacking-stitch down the spine on to the pad, ensuring that the flag will still be visible after the saddle is in place. If the rider is wearing a tail coat, make sure that it does not hide the emblem. Also, do not put the flag cloth too far back, where it may not only irritate the horse but will also give the illusion of a long back.

Finally, before the horse leaves the stable for the last time before his test, you can dust him over. There are many products on sale today that add shine to the horse's coat, but a little baby oil on a rag is just as effective. When using the oil, make sure that there is not too much dust about, because the oil will attract enough dust to make you want to scream! This applies to hoof dressing as well, though you can also use a blacking that is fast-drying and leaves the hooves shiny and black without attracting sand or dirt. It is questionable as to how much good these products do for the hooves but they are certainly effective in enhancing their appearance; also you may find that it is days or even weeks before the blacking wears off.

Rider and groom preparing for the Dressage Test. Note the attention to detail: checker-board pattern on hindquarters, tail bandage kept on until the last possible moment.

Finishing touches. The groom paints the horse's hooves to enhance his appearance in the Dressage Arena.

So, you have done your job; horse and rider are equally immaculate, and off they go towards the Dressage arena. You should then tidy your stable area as quickly as you can and make your way up to the arena. Take with you a bucket containing your quick-repair kit, which will consist of some hoof dressing, a brush, a rub rag and a sponge, and – if you want to be really meticulous – a soap sponge with some saddle soap on it. Add also a rub rag for your rider's boots, to give them a final polish. The most important thing to remember is a fly spray. Even if you think that flies will not be a problem, put some spray on the horse before he leaves the stable and then re-apply it just before he does his test. Wipe it on with a cloth rather than spraying it directly so as not to upset the horse before his test.

Take with you any tack or change of bridle that your rider may have asked for. If you do intend to switch bridles just before the test, don't forget to change the bridle numbers. If it is raining, it is a good idea to take a spare pair of gloves for the rider. Again, if the weather is inclement, take with you some sort of horse sheet or blanket, and a surcingle for the return walk home. Take also the horse's headcollar for leading him back after the test. Finally, you should have ready some kind of titbit, such as a carrot or a piece of sugar for the horse who, you hope, is going to perform like a star. Make sure that you have your groom's pass, and then make your way to the Dressage arena.

The greatest drawback for a groom at a Three-Day Event is that you rarely see very much of the competition. You will be busy with your own horse, and his test will be one of the few that you will see.

Once you arrive at the warm-up area, keep an eye on what is going on. Check which competitor is in the arena, and note the amount of time left before it is your rider's turn to compete. Always be somewhere where your rider can easily see you, so that if he needs any last-minute repairs or a change of studs, he will not have to search you out. Try to keep calm and to have a light-hearted attitude, as this phase of the competition can be nerve-wracking enough for the rider without having to cope with a wound-up groom.

Remember the rules. If your horse is wearing boots or any type of wrap for the warm-up, be sure to remove them before he enters the arena. If necessary, remind the rider to drop his whip, and check that he has not forgotten to wear gloves and spurs. These are all rules which if ignored can mean instant elimination. An official will be present to check that the horse has a legal bit in his mouth and that the rider is wearing blunt spurs; this usually happens about five or ten minutes before the test begins.

At International Events, such as the World Championships and the Olympic Games, there will be two or three practice arenas available to the riders at a certain time before their tests. Usually the last practice arena is out of bounds to everyone, including the groom, so check this beforehand and make sure that all repairs and touching-up jobs are done before horse and rider escape from your clutches! Sometimes the rider will decide that the horse is warming-up well and that to stop for you to apply hoof dressing and an extra polish will only break his rhythm and cause loss of concentration. He will therefore keep moving straight on into the arena, giving you no chance to do anything. Do not let this worry you. It is far more important to produce a horse performing a good accurate test, even though he may not have the shiniest feet in town, than an agitated and unsettled beauty with not a hair out of place.

With horse and rider in the arena, you are now free to allow yourself the nervous excitement of watching. After the test, your job is to attend to the horse's needs; loosen the noseband and girth, give him a treat, and put on a sheet if needed. Even if the test has been a disaster, try to remember some of the good parts, and be constructive; the rider will know his shortcomings better than anyone, and will need your support not your criticisms. So avoid an expression that implies, 'I could have done a better job on a donkey with two legs'. Adopt, rather, the attitude, 'Well, now the worst part is over. With the Cross-Country ahead, it's all fun from now on.'

Probably the next thing that you will do is to take the horse back to the stables. The only out-of-the-ordinary occurrence that may happen is that the horse may at random be chosen for a drug test; this is to make sure that he has not received any illegal substances. The list of horses to be tested is picked out of a hat, so do not suppose that the finger has been pointed at you in particular! Generally, as the horse leaves the arena you will be approached by a vet or his assistant, who will tell you that they wish to collect a sample from your horse. This can be an inconvenience, but they are only doing their job, so full co-operation from you will make everyone's life easier. There may be a stable set aside somewhere for this testing, and

Just before the Dressage Test. The beautifully turned-out horse, complete with neatly plaited mane and pulled tail, looks on as the rider puts on his number. Note the grooming kit ready for any last-minute touching-up.

you will take your horse there immediately. If not, the sample will be collected once you have reached your own stable area.

Whoever is taking the sample will accompany you all the way. They are usually very helpful, understanding people and will often wait until you have untacked your horse and blanketed him. A urine sample is usually all that is needed. However, sometimes the horse does not feel like urinating in front of everyone, in which case, after an hour of waiting, whistling and shaking straw in the hopes of encouraging the horse to relieve himself, the vet will take a blood sample instead. Occasionally he may also take a saliva sample.

Such testing, on a random, unannounced basis, is for the good of the sport, and it protects the horses against drug abuse. Your horse may also be tested after the Cross-Country and after the Show Jumping. In some international competitions the top-placed horses will undergo tests automatically. You will be asked to witness the testing for your own satisfaction, and your signature will be needed after the containers have been sealed.

Having arrived back at the stable with your horse, put him in his stall and untack him. Give him the chance to urinate and roll if he wants to, before you get to work. Then unplait him, take out any studs, and pack the holes. If it is warm enough and if he warrants it, you may wash him down – but use your common sense.

Quite often, if the Cross-Country is on the following day, your rider may wish to give the horse a final 'blow-out' or 'pipe-opener' or 'breeze'. These are all expressions to describe a short sharp gallop that will 'blow out' any 'cobwebs' in the horse's lungs and windpipes. It just sharpens up their respiratory system and gives them that final edge before the big day. So perhaps after your horse has staled and rolled you will need to prepare him for his 'blow out' by putting on the jumping tack and boots. On his return from this outing, cool him out, walk him if necessary, and ration his water intake until he is fully recovered, just as you would at home.

Another task you may have after the Dressage test is that of clipping your horse. As we explained in Chapter 2 (page 26), more and more people prefer to clip just before a Three-Day Event so that the horse will cool down more quickly. Clipping may be done at home, before you leave for the Event, but if you do not want your horse to have a clipped-looking coat for the Dressage, this task will befall you on the night before Cross-Country. It can be a real headache for the groom, not to mention an aggravation for the horse at a time when he should be relaxing and conserving his energies. Should you decide to clip, remember to take enough blankets with you to keep the horse warm. But a word of warning – if you need to tranquillise him in order to get the clippers anywhere near him, you had better forget it entirely – that is if you do not want to be eliminated for using illegal substances.

Preparing for Speed and Endurance

After the horse has completed his Dressage test, and perhaps had a blow-out, and when you have looked after his immediate needs, you can start to gear your thinking towards the next phase – the Speed and Endurance day – and all the preparations that this will entail. You should have already made a detailed study of the course and will know where the Start, the Steeplechase, and the Box are situated. If you don't know these things, now is the time to find out. You must know how long it is going to take you to get to the Start with ample time to spare. Also, you must know whether it will be physically possible to get yourself and some equipment to the Steeplechase or whether, instead, you will need to delegate that job to a helper – so that you will be in the Box for the arrival of your horse and rider after the Second Roads and Tracks.

Let us outline the best plan of attack. First of all, find the start of Phase A. Work out how long it will take you to get the horse there with enough time to allow your rider to weigh-out and re-saddle. Be generous in allotting time for these things. Remember that your normally calm horse may feel the tension and fidget so much at the Start that it becomes a mammoth task just to get the saddle back on. Nothing is worse for everyone's state of mind than a messy and rushed start.

If your rider carries lead, try to find out where the practice scales are. These are normally close to the stable area and will help your rider to judge how much lead he will need early on, instead of juggling with weights ten minutes before the off.

Next we come to the Steeplechase. How far away is it? Is it within easy walking distance? Don't forget to allow for spectator congestion and for the fact that you will be carrying a bucket full of equipment. If it is not within easy walking distance, can you be reasonably sure that you can drive there and arrive in time to be of assistance should your rider need any before the start of the Steeplechase? Will you be able to obtain appropriate passes that will get you to where you want to be without being stopped by officials? More important, can you get to the Box area in time to set up your equipment before your rider's arrival? These are all calculations that must be made well in advance. Do not leave anything to chance. If there is any possibility that you will not be able to make it to both the Steeplechase and the Box, then you must arrange for someone responsible to cover the Steeplechase, so that you will be free to be in the Box.

Next, go to the Box and check out the facilities there. Know where the end of Phase C and the start of Phase D are sited. Pick a spot that you think will be a good place in which to work on your horse. If it is going to be hot, choose a place that affords shade. In bad weather, pick an area sheltered from the wind. Remember that tomorrow you will not be the only one in the Box; so if your horse is likely to be particularly difficult – such as kicking out – in situations such as these, try to be in a spot where you will be out of harm's way and not endangering anyone else. Find out exactly what facilities will be available. As a general rule, most Three-Day Events have plenty of water. However, in some cases it will only be suitable for washing and not for drinking, so be prepared to bring your own. In the hotter climes, ice will even be supplied. There is usually a blacksmith and always at least one vet available. But, double check! Should it be cold on Cross-Country day, it is preferable to have warm water for washing down. Many people have some sort of insulated water-carrier; if you don't, use a regular container and fill it with really hot water just before you take your equipment to the Box area.

You will also need to know when all your equipment has to be at the Box. In some cases the officials will allow you to drive right up and unload everything whenever you want to; but often getting to the Box involves crossing the course, and the organisers will set a deadline for the driving of vehicles there. Find out! If any of your plans entail driving, make sure that you have the correct passes to take you where you need to go with the least difficulty.

Now, with all this store of information you can return to the stables and start preparing for Cross-Country day. Start with the equipment for the Steeplechase. This should be kept simple, remembering that in most cases you will have to cart it over to the Box. Take a bucket in which to carry

Ice, as well as water, is often supplied in the Box (especially in summer) to help cool out hot horses after the Cross-Country.

everything. Sometimes there will be water at the end of the Steeplechase – find out. If it is not available, and the weather is hot, you might like to have water with you so that you can cool your horse down quickly as he finishes Phase B. For this you will also need a sponge and a towel. If there is to be a blacksmith at the end of B take spare shoes. If not, take shoe-pulling tools, Elastoplast, and an Easyboot, in case your horse spreads or loses a shoe. In such an emergency these items should get your horse safely to the Box, where a blacksmith will be able to replace the shoe. Take a headcollar with you, too, in case there is a hold-up on the course, or in case something happens that entails your having to lead the horse back to the stables. This may be unfortunate but it is quite possible, and we strongly believe that if you are prepared it will not happen! You should also take with you a small emergency first-aid kit and, if you have room, a sheet of some sort. It is a good idea to carry an assortment of tools in your pockets, such as a hoof pick, a wrench, a selection of studs, a pair of scissors, hole punchers, and some insulating tape. Include, also, an extra pair of reins and a spare leather and iron, in case of a mishap on Phase A or B.

With your equipment for the Steeplechase all ready, now assemble the things you will need for the Box. We suggest that you take the following:

For the horse
Waterproof sheet (can be used to cover all the equipment in bad weather)
Headcollar and leadline
3 Water buckets
2 Large body sponges
Small sponge for washing out mouth
Sweat scraper
Plenty of towels
Anti-sweat sheet
Cooler
Surcingle
Grease
Rubber gloves (for use when applying grease)
Spare set of shoes, with studs already in place
Stud box
Hoof pick
Selection of spare boots and bandages
Talcum powder
Spare bridle
Extra pair of reins

Spare girth
Spare overgirth
Saddle pad
Spare leathers and irons
Spare jumping saddle (not a necessity, but a good idea if you have one; if it is a wet day, the rider will appreciate a dry saddle before cross-country – but be sure the weights are adjusted, where necessary)
Small first-aid kit
Pair of scissors
Pair of hole punchers
Quick repair kit (insulating tape, safety pins, elastic bands, needles and thread)

For the rider
Coat or warm jacket
Drink
Dry gloves
Spare whip and spurs
Programme with a map of the course

All equipment should be packed in a trunk or a large tote bag. The above list is very comprehensive, but it is most important to be prepared for all eventualities.

Apart from the items that you will be using on the morning of Cross-Country, everything for the trip to the Steeplechase and to the Box should now be packed and ready for you to pick up and take with you on the following day.

Next, turn your attention to the tack that the horse will be wearing. Go over all the stitching again, and double-check that the billets and buckles are all secure. Obviously a thorough tack check should have been carried out long before you arrived at the Event, so this final check is more for your peace of mind. Should you find a couple of stitches not quite as secure as you would like, you can either replace the piece of tack with a spare part you will have brought with you, or you can do some last-minute repairs yourself. If you are planning to change the bridle or saddle in the Box, make sure now that the replacements fit correctly and are adjusted to your

Preparing and loading the equipment for the Box on the evening before Speed and Endurance Day is a great time-saver and leaves you with less to worry about.

horse's requirements, rather than trying to alter a new bridle on the day – bad planning that simply asks for trouble.

As you are checking everything that your horse will be wearing, don't forget to include the shoes. If there is a blacksmith readily available, then do get him to check the shoes as a matter of course, even if you are satisfied with their fit and tightness. Shoes are a major factor in a Three-Day Event and it is vital for the groom to be aware of their condition at all times. For example, there was the case of *Better and Better* at Lexington in 1982. The horse had been shod one week before the competition. The clenches were checked and tightened the night before Cross-Country, and so he set off on Phase A with perfect shoes. As he came off Phase A, everything was fine. As he finished the Steeplechase, the groom checked them again, and they were on snugly, with all the studs in place. She started to wash him off quickly before he set out on Phase C, when he trod on the inside of one of his hind shoes and completely pulled it away from the foot. Fortunately a blacksmith was on the spot. The shoe was removed and replaced, and off he went, finishing clean and fast with no further trouble. Had no one noticed this, he would have cut the opposite leg to ribbons with the protruding metal.

The weather, and the condition of the footing, will determine which studs your rider will require in the shoes. To save time and trouble if a horse loses a shoe, it is a good idea to put the same type of studs in the spare shoes. By so doing, you will not have to waste time screwing in studs after the blacksmith has put the shoe on.

Having checked the tack, make sure that you have collected enough grooms' passes and time sheets for all your helpers.

To make quite sure that you have covered everything, you should have a meeting that night between yourself, your rider, and anyone else who will be helping you. This is essential, to clarify each individual's job. Underline how important each person is, even if all they are doing is holding the horse or making sure the rider gets a drink in the Box. A team is only as strong as its weakest member, and if you have done your homework methodically your team will have no weakness. Make sure that all your helpers know where the Box and the Steeplechase areas are situated. Run over the rules that are important, such as not helping the rider to dismount after Cross-Country – which could eliminate him. Arrange for everyone to meet up again the next day for a final briefing.

Now you have planned away as much of Cross-Country day as you can. The equipment is packed. The water containers, if needed, are ready to be filled. Everyone has a time sheet and a pretty clear idea of what is expected of them the next day. All the tack is safe and clean, and the horse's shoes are tightly secure. It is time to turn your attention, once again, to the horse.

On the night before Cross-Country special consideration must be given to the horse's feed and hay. Many people, especially if their Cross-Country is early in the day, will only give the horse a small evening meal and will cut back on the hay. This is to ensure that there is not a great amount of bulk still being digested inside the horse during the competition, thus precluding valuable blood vessel activity from being concentrated in the gut; maximum use of the circulatory system is needed to carry oxygen to all parts of the body as the horse stretches itself to one hundred per cent activity. Similarly, he must not be so full of hay, feed or water that his lungs cannot expand to full capacity, thus restricting his oxygen intake.

So feed a light supper and a reduced amount of hay – perhaps one flake – no later than six or seven o'clock. If your horse is bedded on straw, and you think that he may eat it during the night, use a muzzle. You can buy excellent ones that do not rub or cause sweating and yet still allow the horse to drink water. It is not as cruel as it may seem – as you will know if you have ever seen a horse that has 'blown up' half way round the Steeplechase because his stomach was full of straw and he could not get enough oxygen.

We will discuss watering in the next chapter, so we will not go into detail here, except to say that in the hotter climates it is advisable to feed electrolytes. These are a mixture of essential trace minerals and salts that the body loses with excessive sweating, and that need replacing. You can buy them anywhere, but it is best to consult your own vet, who will be able to tell you how much and when to feed them for each particular horse, according to the climate and the work involved. These additives can be put either into the feed or into the water. If you choose to put them in the usual water bucket, be sure to have a second bucket filled with pure water only.

It is a good idea to take the horse out for a hand walk just before you put him away for the night. This will allow him to stretch his legs and it will give him the opportunity to pick at some grass and to relax. By this stage in the game, everyone, including the horses, can feel the tension beginning to build up.

A final word about legs. Many people firmly believe in putting some sort of tightening liniment on the horse's legs the night before Cross-Country, just to tighten everything up and to cool the legs out a little. This should be discussed with your rider.

So put your horse away – warmly blanketed if you have clipped him, muzzled if he is a pig on straw, and legs wrapped, either for protection and warmth, or with some sort of astringent. You are now finished for the day, except for a late-night check to make sure he is comfortable.

You should now be all set and confident about tomorrow. No one can deny that it will be the most nerve-wracking twenty-four hours in the whole week for you. You will need a good night's rest because, even if things go really well for you during the day, tomorrow night will be long and tiring. If things go badly, it can be fraught with disappointments and sadness. So, have a decent meal, go to bed early, and try to get straight to sleep.

CHAPTER EIGHT

The Three-Day Event: Speed and Endurance

Preparing the Horse

Cross-Country Day is the most important twenty-four hours of any Event for you and your team. For those who are not lacking in imagination it will certainly have its tense moments, so the more planning you have done in advance, the more confident and efficient you will be. Any nervousness should be due more to concentration and concern for your horse and rider than to worries about unchecked tack breaking, or similar disasters.

Obviously your schedule will largely depend on your horse's starting times. Be sure to arrive at the stables as early as possible. Today is the one day when you should allow a generous amount of time for each task, so do not try to cut things too fine.

Muck out and check that the horse is well and has incurred no injury during the night. At least four hours before the start of Phase A give the horse just a small feed, so that he can digest it quickly and easily. If he is the type to eat anything that is put in front of him, you can give him some electrolytes; if not, do not risk putting him off his feed, and just give him an undoctored breakfast. In order to avoid a problem such as colic it is important that the horse should have something going through his system. If a horse has absolutely nothing in his stomach and then exerts himself to a point where he is dehydrated – as many Event horses are after the Speed and Endurance test (especially in the hotter climates) – there is a risk of abdominal problems, as the walls may stick together because of lack of moisture and food matter. On the other hand, you certainly do not want a horse with a stomach full of hay and feed just before Cross-Country. So, at this time, forget the hay and just give a small feed – probably no more than two pounds of grain. All water should be removed a full hour before the off.

Now is the time to fill any water containers that you will need and to drive them with all the other equipment up to the Box. If you will be using hot water, you can add it at the last minute. Usually water supplied at Events comes in tankers, most often with practically no pressure. So avoid the possibility of having to wait in line as everyone tries to fill their buckets at the same time, right in the middle of the day. It is better to do this before you have to start preparing the horse and while the Box area is quiet and not hemmed in by spectators. Now is an ideal time to show your helpers where to find everything. It is always easier to explain what is required of them if you are actually on the spot, pointing out things like the start box, where the vets are likely to be, and where to catch first sight of horse and rider on their way to the Box from Phase C.

Choose your spot carefully, remembering to pick a sheltered place if it is very hot, windy, or raining. It is helpful to be not too far from the starting area, so that there will be no difficulty hearing the officials call for your rider or counting down the precious ten minutes. A trunk is probably the easiest receptacle in which to stow all your equipment. Failing that, use a large canvas or nylon tote bag. You must keep everything in one place and thus cut down the chance of losing things in your hurry to get back to the stables at the end of the day.

Take a rainproof sheet with you to throw over all your belongings. This will keep everything dry while you are at the stables and Steeplechase, and will deter people from borrowing your equipment.

By now you should have worked out if you need someone else to do the checking at the start and finish of the Steeplechase, so that you are free to go to the Box. There should be no more than three people, including yourself, around the horse in the Box. Any more will just lead to confusion and wasted time. Even two people will suffice if the horse is well behaved and as long as they both know what they are doing. Plan your strategy for the Box in detail – from who holds the horse right down to exactly how many minutes before the 'off' your rider will want to get mounted. Write all these things down and have a copy posted in the tack room for everyone to refer to; and keep a copy also with you at all times. Once everyone has been briefed and the grooms' passes have been handed out (these guarantee free access to designated areas), now is perhaps the time to have a final run through with your rider – just to re-confirm, for your mutual benefit, the plan for the day.

Before you start preparing the horse, lay out any equipment that you will need back at the stables after the Cross-Country is all over. Put out bandages and poultices, and if you plan to give him a complete bath, lay out the washing-down equipment. You should also include anti-sweat sheets, blankets, a small haynet, and a bran mash. This preparation will be of great help to you when you return; everything will be at hand and, should there be a disaster of some kind you will have time to concentrate on it rather than having to worry about where you put the newspaper for the poultice.

A word about poultices. There are two ways of applying these – either hot or cold. A **hot poultice** is very useful in restoring circulation and therefore in helping the healing process for damaged areas with scar tissue that needs to be broken down; it is also useful for drawing out infection. However, putting something hot on legs that may be bruised will only encourage the blood vessels to dilate, and this will increase the haemorrhaging (bruising). With human skin, a bruise appears as a reddish blue mark; with horses the only way we have of finding out is by feeling and looking for swellings. Legs and tendons are tender to the touch immediately after bruising has occurred; swelling may take up to a day to appear, especially as your horse is likely to be somewhat dehydrated and therefore lacking in the fluids that produce a swelling. In this instance we would advise you to play safe by using a **cold poultice**. This will immediately constrict the blood vessels and will arrest any haemorrhaging, thus keeping the bruised tissue to a minimum. It will also draw out any heat caused by concussion from the hard ground or by jolts at drop fences. It really is a matter of your own judgment, your horse's particular needs, and your assessment of the most suitable type of treatment.

If you are planning to use a hot poultice, arrange now for the means of warming it up; many people carry a portable burner with them. If you are using a cold poultice, and a refrigerator is not available, leave the can sitting in a bucket of ice all day. Or if there is an ice cream seller nearby, perhaps he can be persuaded to help!

Sometimes if the ground is hard and your horse is susceptible to bruised soles, it is a good idea to pack the feet. You can only do this if your horse is not wearing pads, as the packing must go directly on to the foot. There are a number of packings on the market, but a good mud-type poultice is excellent. All you have to do is fill the concave hollow of each foot with the packing until it is flush with the edge of the shoes. Then you can slap a piece of brown paper over it to keep it protected. You do not have to secure it in any way, as it will dry and stay in the foot, just like mud. This is best done once the horse is in the stall for the night, so that he does not walk too much and loosen it. It will draw out any heat and generally soothe the foot. In the morning, all you need is a hoof pick to remove it. This packing procedure may be done regularly if the ground is always hard, or if your horse is sensitive, or always carries a little heat in his feet.

The next procedure on your list should be to take your horse for a hand walk to keep his muscles warm and moving. Twenty minutes is ample. Try to keep him away from all the bustle and excitement, so that he does not waste energy by leaping around and getting himself wound up. Remember, you have a fighting fit animal on your hands, so do not take any chances. Lead him out in a bridle if necessary, and let him pick at a little grass if it will help to relax him.

Once this is done, set out all the tack you need. If your horse wears boots, dust the insides with talcum powder to avoid rubs. If he wears bandages, prepare all the necessary wrappings. Have a bootlace ready for securing the bridle. Lay out the studs and the tools for them. If your rider likes to ride with the mane braided, add the plaiting equipment. This is up to the rider. Some prefer the mane loose so that it is available should they want to grab a handful over a particularly difficult or unseating fence. Others prefer the mane out of the way of their hands so that there is no chance of getting their fingers trapped in it.

The next task is to give your horse a quick groom. Turnout is not of major importance today, so do not spend too much time fiddling around the horse. He will need as much peace and quiet as you can allow him.

Next put in road studs. This should be an easy task if you have previously packed the stud holes with oiled cotton wool. If the horse is bedded on straw and you have muzzled him during the night to prevent him from eating it, keep the muzzle on or tie the horse up. It would be silly to allow him the chance to guzzle quantities of straw now, after depriving him of it all night. This may seem harsh, but if you cannot bed him on shavings or peat, it really is acting in his interests.

After you have plaited the horse and put in the studs, you can then fit the boots on. Many riders like to do this themselves. If you are not totally confident about your ability to put on boots or bandages for such a long endurance test, it is better for the rider to do the job. It is so easy to damage tendons – albeit unintentionally – by putting boots or bandages on too tightly, or so loosely that they slip and then tighten around the leg. Bandaging takes time and practice, and the tension-filled surroundings of Cross-Country day are not the ideal place in which to start learning. Your rider will certainly not condemn you for asking him to do the job if you are not one hundred per cent sure.

If *you* are putting on the boots, remember to use ones that have been worn-in and will not stretch. Also, be sure that they have previously been used by this particular horse, so that there are no last-minute panics with boots that do not fit. Remember, also, that boots and bandages are intended for protection. If they are too tight they will cut down the circulation, which can damage tissues and tendons through depriving these parts of blood and oxygen when it is most needed – at full exertion.

If you are using bandages, do not pull them too tightly, and make sure they are securely finished off. Most people sew the end of the bandage down, which is probably the best method. Others use sticky tape, which we do not consider to be reliable, especially if the horse has to negotiate water jumps or if conditions are wet and muddy. Always bandage the legs by unrolling the wrap from the front, around the outside to the back, and back to the front via the inside, keeping the bandage close to the leg, to prevent you from pulling too tightly. Try always to finish at the top on the outside, even if it means cutting the bandage; this is the least likely place for it to get caught on anything and ripped off.

Over-reach or bell boots are, in our opinion, essential equipment. You may disagree because in muddy conditions the boots just become full of mud and add to the weight that the horse has to contend with. Again, it is up to your rider. If you do use them, remember that they are not supposed to fit snugly around the pastern, as this causes rubs. You should be able comfortably to poke a finger down under the top of a bell boot.

The next stage is to tack up. If your rider carries lead, your schedule may have a variation here. With or without lead, all competitors are required to

Rider weighing-out before the start of Phase A.

Many riders have to carry lead to make the minimum weight. Having spare lead ready in the area near the scales can save time and anxiety during those tense minutes before the start.

weigh-out. This is to make sure that all riders are carrying the minimum weight of 75 kilograms (11st. 11lbs. or 165lbs). At some Events they may weigh-out before they start and are then allowed to go back to the stables to tack up. In this case they need to go down to the start of Phase A only at their departure time. The more important the competition, the less likely they are to be allowed such freedom. After all, if you were really devious, you could weigh-out with the correct amount, then remove the lead, and ride under weight; as long as the scales showed the correct weight at the end of Phase D, no one would know. In theory, this is quite possible, though we have never heard of anyone trying it, and we would hope that the ethics of Eventers are above such dastardly deeds!

Generally you will find that once having arrived at the start of Phase A the officials will expect the rider to weigh-out, tack up, and then start – all within sight of them.

Using the practice scales which are usually provided in the stable area, your rider may weigh himself and calculate how much lead he will or will not need to carry. In *theory* this should make for a much easier life, because it means that the weigh-out at the Start is just a formality. Do not believe it! We have been to more than one big Three-Day Event where the practice scales and the scales at the Start were not synchronised with each other. Last-minute mad panics – pulling lead out or, worse still, finding more to stuff quickly into the weight pad – can be avoided if someone makes sure that both sets of scales work correctly, or are at least on level ground. Be prepared by taking a couple of extra pounds of lead to the Start with you. Most riders will weigh-out a pound or two over at the beginning to compensate for their own weight loss during the ride.

Finish tacking up by tying with a bootlace the headpiece of the bridle into a plait behind the horse's ear. This is to prevent the bridle being pulled off should your rider have the misfortune to fall off over the horse's head, thus avoiding the loss of time chasing a loose and bridleless horse around the park. Many people laugh at this use of a simple bootlace, but we know it works, strange as a single plait and a bow may look. Anyway, you would feel a complete idiot if you scornfully refused to do this and the bridle *did* come off in a fall.

You are now almost ready to leave the stables with your horse. He is as prepared as he will ever be. Cast a last glance around to make sure that you have not forgotten anything. Everything that you could possibly need for your return should be assembled and waiting. The equipment for the Box is already in place. All your helpers are well briefed and on their way to their stations. Your pockets are full of the tools that you may need.

If you are going to the Start, you should have the bucket of gear for the Steeplechase with you. Put some sort of blanket over your horse to lead him to the Start, and have his headcollar on. If for any reason the start is delayed, it is only wise to have a blanket to keep the horse warm, and a headcollar so that you are not continually pulling him around by his mouth.

If there are going to be large crowds, it is a good idea for someone to accompany you to the Start. This assistant will help to clear a way through the throngs of spectators who may not be used to seeing a horse actually walking along beside them and are often slow to move out of the way.

Phase A. First Roads and Tracks

Arrive at the Start about twenty minutes before the off. This should give your rider time to weigh-out, put the saddle back on, mount and make any adjustments, and for you to secure the overgirth. Should your rider be one of those wisps of a girl who carry twice their own weight in lead it is a good idea to allow yourselves more time at the Start for settling all the pads in their right place. It is also worth enlisting the help of a strong, tall man who will lift the weights on to the horse.

With your rider up in the saddle you are now waiting for the signal to start. Should your horse be very excited by this whole performance, it may be necessary for you to lead him around and even into the starting box.

All systems go! Horse and rider wait quietly for the Timekeeper to give them the count-down.

This is perfectly legal. You are allowed to hold the horse until the start signal is given, when you must then let go. Ideally you should use a leather line which you can slip through the bit and which can easily be removed by letting it go at one end and allowing it to slip out effortlessly and without disturbing the horse. Make no attempt to do anything but hold the horse. If you unthinkingly slap the horse on its rump when the official says 'go', you may find that you have eliminated your rider by giving 'outside assistance'.

Once your rider is on Phase A, you have anything from twelve to twenty-five minutes to get yourself over to the start of the Steeplechase. This will present no problems to a groom who has done her homework, who knows the way, and who has not forgotten her groom's pass. You should arrive at the Steeplechase area well before your rider. If there is to be a blacksmith there, find him so that you know in advance where he is. Know the direction from which your rider will be appearing, and keep your eyes peeled. Most riders will arrive from Phase A with at least a couple of

Horse and rider proceed along the Roads and Tracks, Phase A, that lead to the Steeplechase, Phase B.

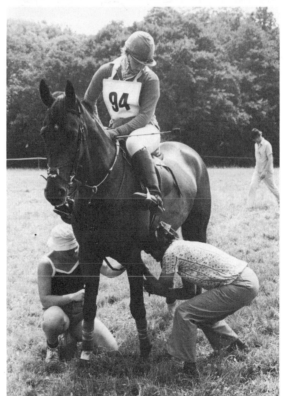

Most riders finish Phase A early, thus allowing time in the neutral zone for the groom to adjust the girth, etc, before the start of the Steeplechase.

Action up-front on the Steeplechase. Action behind-the-scenes should show the same kind of vigour and determination.

minutes in hand, to allow for a check of the girth, to hitch up the stirrups, and perhaps to watch some of the other competitors ride the course.

Phase B. Steeplechase

If the Steeplechase is held on very slippery ground, you may have to change over to larger studs with very little time to spare. Don't panic. It is just a matter of unscrewing one set and putting in another. If the horse is well behaved it will only take a couple of minutes. If the horse is a stranger to you, or known to be a fidget, your rider must allow extra time and you should change the most vital studs first, working from the back to the front.

As the rider approaches the end of Phase A, stand close to the Finish so that you can immediately check the horse's shoes. This job – in good weather at any rate – can be done by just watching the horse from behind as it moves away from you. There is no need to pick up each foot unless you really cannot see or if you are in any doubt. Then, from the bottom up, look carefully for anything that is not right. Make sure that he has all his shoes – which usually means that you will have been able to see all the studs as well. Are all the boots and bandages secure? Check the girth and the overgirth; if you tighten them, pull the horse's forelegs out to prevent any pinching. If necessary, lead the horse around until his time is called for the start of Phase B. Here the same rules apply for starting as they did at Phase A. You might just remind your rider to punch his watch before you lead him into the starting box; from there it is safer not to say anything.

In the neutral zone at the end of the Steeplechase (before the start of Phase C, Second Roads and Tracks) the horse can be quietly checked over and refreshed.

Phase C. Second Roads and Tracks

There is usually not much time for you to get to the end of the Steeplechase course, unless it is in the same place as the Start, which is fairly unusual. You should have worked out your route to the finish of Phase B so that you can get there without being turned back by officials and without crossing the course in a dangerous place.

At all Events there is an area after the end of the Steeplechase where riders are allowed assistance, should they need it. It is usually some way from the actual Finish, giving your rider ample time in which to pull up quietly. This is your chance to check that no damage has been done. Arrange for the rider to trot towards you, to check that the horse is sound. If the ground is hard, horses will often appear to be lame when they first come off the course. This is some sort of 'sting' that most of them seem to walk out of, so, unless your horse seems to be favouring one leg in particular, or he seems to be really stiff behind (meaning that he may be tieing-up), do not worry unduly. Given a few minutes into Phase C he should recover.

As your rider is allowed to stop, you may take this opportunity to check

All the necessary equipment is set out in the Box, ready for the horse's arrival after Phase C.

After passing through the finish of Phase C the dismounted rider trots the horse up towards the Panel at the entrance to the 10-minute compulsory halt area, the Box.

the shoes again. If there is some work to be done on them and there is a blacksmith available, go ahead and have the spread or lost shoe replaced. If not, you will have time to put a temporary Easyboot on the offending foot until the blacksmith in the Box can put the shoe back on again. If all is well, and the weather permits, sponge the horse's mouth and neck. You can afford about a couple of minutes for this if no drastic repairs are necessary. Loosen the girths by one hole, and the noseband, to make the horse more comfortable on Phase C. Offer the rider a drink. Then collect all your equipment and head on towards the Box.

The Ten-Minute Box before the Cross-Country phase

For you the most important part of the Event is about to take place. We cannot deny that, even for someone who has done this job for years, the butterflies just do not subside. As long as you don't allow your nerves to get such a hold on you that you can't do your job satisfactorily, you will be fine. You will have already covered the next ten minutes a thousand times in your head – even dreamed about it. The well-being – and success – of your horse and rider must now be uppermost in the minds of you and all your helpers. During this short but vital break you must work quickly, efficiently and quietly around the horse.

When you arrive at the Box, lay all your equipment out on top of the rain sheet. Empty the warm water into the buckets and check that it is at the right temperature. Keep all the washing-down equipment a little way away from the rest of your gear, to prevent things getting wet or being stepped on. The equipment that you will be using should be within easy reach, with the spare tack further away. This will avoid having to scramble over a heap of items when, for instance, you are reaching for a towel. Check the time, and let all your helpers know how long it will be before the rider will appear.

Although you should all know what time your rider is due to start on Phase D, it is a good idea to delegate this job to perhaps a parent or an owner. Usually the time-keepers will give you first a five-minute call, and then one every minute. Good and reliable as these people generally are, they have two or three riders to cope with at the same time. In the rush of the moment, there could be a slip-up – either you might not hear them, or they could omit to give you your time-check. Therefore, having a friend solely in charge of the times – who will give you a time-check every half-minute – will be of great comfort and help. In team competitions this task is often carried out by the coach.

Check that all the equipment is assembled and waiting and that your helpers are at the ready. You will now probably have about ten minutes before the rider comes in from Phase C. The Box will look very different today from yesterday. It will be full of other competitors and their helpers and there will be a large crowd of onlookers peering over the barriers. It is easy for you to lose someone in the mêlée, and equally easy for the rider not to spot you or your helpers. You should, therefore, wait at the Finish of Phase C so that you can lead the horse back to your area. Most riders will come in from Phase C between two and five minutes early, to give the horse a longer period of rest in the Box. This time is very precious, and you must make the very most of it. Be ready for an early arrival. As the rider comes into the Box there will be an examination by officials, including a vet, who will thoroughly but rapidly check the horse for lameness, injury, or excessive tiredness.

To save time, the rider will probably trot the last twenty yards on a loose rein towards the judges, to show that the horse is sound. This will obviate the need to trot him up again, thus saving time and energy. The Panel will most likely take the horse's pulse, temperature and respiration, depending on the climate and the animal's condition as he arrives; this is a very necessary part of the competition. Do not attempt to interfere at this point. The officials fully realise that you are anxious to save time and get to work on the horse, but they have their job to do, which is in the best interests of the horse.

Having completed this formality at the end of Phase C the rider will then go straight to his trainer, and/or his personal helper, where he can have a breather and a drink, and get an up-date on how the course is riding. At this stage he should not have to do anything with the horse, which should be solely your responsibility. The rider should feel confident that the horse will get the best treatment in the shortest time; this means allowing the horse the maximum time to walk around, catch his breath, and be in the best possible condition before the start of Phase D.

So at the end of Phase C you are at the Finish line waiting. As he trots by, if you have time, look to see that all the shoes are on and all the studs are in. If there is not time, the shoes should be the first items to check when you get back to your working area.

Your rider will jump off while you loosen the noseband and put on the headcollar. If you are going to change bridles, the whole bridle can now come off. (Do not forget to undo the bootlace!) Unless your horse is an angel and there are no martingales to get tangled up in, it really is not

When the rider has dismounted, the vets check the horse's vital signs. Note that the groom is at hand and will lose no time in getting to work.

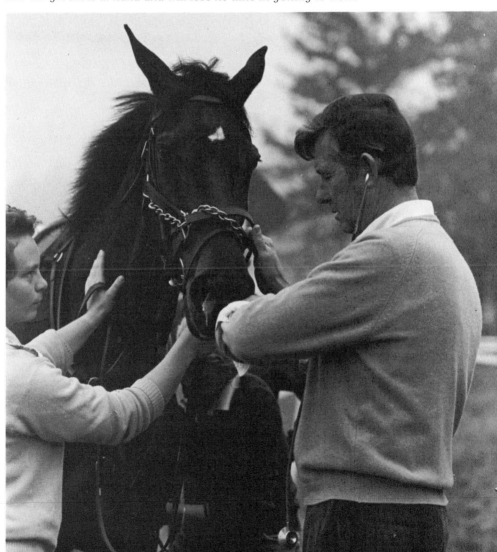

worth taking the bridle off at this point. It wastes time that can otherwise be used profitably in leading the horse around.

When you loosen any straps, make a mental note of where they were secured, so that you can do them up in the same place later on. If your bridle has a removable flash attachment, for goodness sake do it up so that it does not fall off as you lead the horse around.

While you are putting on the headcollar and the vets are checking the horse, one of your helpers should be taking off the saddle. The only reasons for *not* taking off the saddle are (a) if there is a lot of lead in the pad that may make a quick tacking-up job impossible or risky, or (b) if the horse is particularly difficult to work around and will not stand still for more than two seconds; in this case it is safer for everyone and far less aggravating for the horse if the saddle is just left alone. If for either of these reasons, you *do* leave the saddle on you will probably have to undo the girths and to readjust the saddle should it have slipped back – which often happens. Anyway, this is something you should have discussed the previous day with your rider, weighing the pros and cons and taking the safest way. So, now you can lead the horse back to your area, unless . . .

. . . the horse lost a shoe on the Steeplechase, and because there was no blacksmith there you did a temporary repair job with Elastoplast and an

Close-up of a helper changing studs.

There is always a farrier in the Box for any emergency shoeing. Note the 'mud tail' and the rug keeping the horse's hindquarters warm, which is very important when there is a nip in the air.

Easyboot. If so, you should have sought out the blacksmith in the Box the minute you arrived there, have given him the spare shoe, and have advised him of the time your horse was due in.

Or perhaps the horse lost a shoe on Phase C, which calls for very swift action. With such emergencies in mind, the shoes should be easily accessible in your lay-out of equipment. While you throw a blanket of some sort over the horse and check that everything else is all right, your helper should grab the shoes and find the blacksmith. A cast shoe at this stage is most unsatisfactory from both your point of view and that of the horse, as he will not have the benefit of being washed down and walked. However, in no way will he be able to go on to Phase D with only three shoes, so you have to be instantly ready to put things right.

While the shoe is being replaced, keep the horse as comfortable as you can. If it is hot, try to position him in the shade while the blacksmith is working on him. On the other hand do not let him catch a chill.

If there have been no such unfortunate setbacks, follow your planned routine. The vets have checked your horse, you have loosened his bridle, the headcollar is on him and the saddle has been removed. You can now lead him back to your area of the Box and hand him to a helper whose sole job is to hold the horse while you and one other person are working around him. This may sound a pointless task, but it is essential that someone should be there who has nothing else to think about but keeping the horse still. It will make your job easier and therefore the horse will be more quickly refreshed. The holder must be careful to keep the reins, the breast-plate and the martingale out of the way of the water and grease. The best way to hold a horse still is as with race horses – one hand on either side of the bridle, while standing directly in front of him.

Position the horse away from all your equipment and away from any other horse. Though your animal may not kick or move around, there are others who do, so have a place where you will all be out of harm's way. If you are not satisfied with your earlier inspection, quickly, but quietly, so as not to upset the horse, check the boots, shoes and studs. If you plan on

Action in the Box. The groom is washing down the horse quickly but calmly. A helper has the headcollar over the bridle and is taking care to keep the reins well away from the water and grease.

removing the boots do it now, or if a boot needs adjusting, attend to it. If the boots or bandages look good at this point it may not be necessary to take them off unless there is definitely grit down between the leg and the boot. Some people take the boots off to dry them. Again, it is up to your rider and yourself. Be logical, and remember how quickly ten minutes can fly by.

After all the boots and shoes have been checked – which should take about twenty seconds – you can start washing down. In hot weather the point of the exercise is to bring the temperature down as quickly as possible, so be generous with the water. In cold weather the horse will still be hot and you must cool him down –but you must be very careful not to give him a chill. Under no circumstances should you wash the loin area immediately behind the saddle, where the big muscles must be kept warm. If you douse them with cold water you will probably do more harm than good, encouraging cramps and therefore muscle damage. In *hot weather* the places to concentrate on are the head, the throat area, up between the hind legs, the legs, and the neck. In *colder weather* just wash the very sweaty areas as quickly as you can: enough to

Sometimes it is preferable not to remove the saddle before washing down, as a lead weight cloth can be a time-consuming item to replace in a hurry. Note the concentration and team-work of the groom and helpers.

123

make the horse comfortable but not taking so long that he will catch cold.

While you are washing the horse the helper who has removed the saddle for you can follow up with a sweat scraper. When you have finished washing you can then go over the horse with the towels, quickly rubbing off all excess water; this is essential in the colder climates or in cooler weather, but not so important in the heat of an American summer. Use a smaller sponge to wash out the horse's mouth, which will refresh him. Then clean away the dried saliva. (If you cannot manage to do this without having a fight it is better to leave it alone.)

Spongeing the horse's mouth out is vital, no matter what the weather. It should be done quickly but calmly so as not to upset the horse. Note all the equipment neatly arranged and easily accessible.

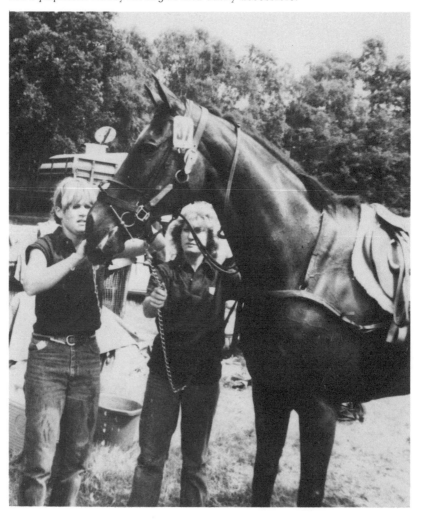

If it is necessary, and if there is time, remove and wash the boots. Here the legs are being dried and the boots replaced.

Throw a sheet, or whatever is practical, over the horse, and if there is a breeze that may blow the sheet around, use a surcingle. Now you can lead the horse about to dry him off and to help him relax and regain his breath. *This walking is essential to help his recovery.* All in all, no more than four minutes should have elapsed between the horse's arrival and your walk-around with him. If the weather is really hot, you can let the horse take one gulp of water, but absolutely *no more.*

It is vital to keep your eye on the time. Ask your appointed clock-watcher to give you a time-check every thirty seconds, so that you know how long you have before the start of Phase D. There are two points to bear in mind here. One is that the panel of judges will most likely want to check the horse again to see that he has recovered satisfactorily and can continue. The other is that the saddle still has to be replaced. Some riders adjust their stirrups before the Cross-Country. This is a job the rider should see to, unless you can trust one of your helpers to do it while you are leading the horse around. We consider it best to replace the saddle first, and then to have the vets check the horse.

If your rider has arrived in the Box with some time in hand your horse will have an extra minute or two in which to recover. When there are about five minutes left before the off, start to put the saddle back on the horse. Your holder should be at the horse's head while you and the other helper put the saddle on. This is where good homework can save valuable time. We, in fact, often show our helpers how to tack up the day before. It may seem a simple exercise, but in the heat of the moment questions such as 'Does the breastplate do up on to the girth-straps or the rings?', 'Does the girth do up on the first two girth-straps, or the first and last?', and 'Where does the surcingle go – under or over the stirrup leather thong?' can all waste time and you would have been better off doing the whole thing yourself. It is not the fault of your helper if she does not know your rider's little likes and dislikes, and it is up to you to see that situations like this do not occur. Make the most of the help; they can be such an asset to your

A rare, quiet moment in the Box as the recovered horse awaits the resting rider. The groom checks her watch as the starting time approaches.

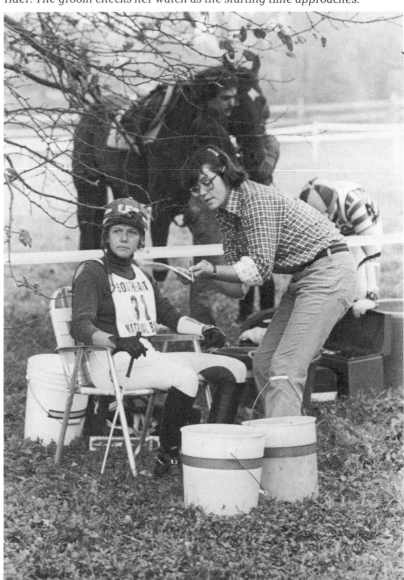

Horse and rider, duly refreshed, await the start of the Cross-Country. While the rider double checks her watch against the times (on a card fixed round her wrist) the groom dries the reins so that they will not be slippery.

team. They really want to be useful, so give them the information that will enable them to help you and your horse.

Having put the saddle back on, throw a sweat sheet over the horse's quarters and continue to lead him round. If they have not approached you yet, ask the panel to check your horse again. Three to four minutes before the off, remove the blanket, tighten the girth and put the rider up on the horse.

Your last task is to apply the grease. This may be Vaseline, lard, or udder balm. You put it on fairly thickly, from high up on the stifles right down to the ground. Of course, it is only the front of the legs that are likely to come in contact with the fences. Many riders believe that the grease enables a horse to slip over any fence that he may hit, and helps him to land on his feet rather than in a pile on the ground. It also helps to prevent scrapes and bruises to the knees and stifles – which are the most common injuries in Horse Trials. It looks ridiculous, but it works; if you have ever walked

Grease has been applied thickly over the front of all four legs, covering the boots and feet, to help the horse if he should hit a fence.

around a course after Cross-Country Day you will have seen just how much grease is left on the fences.

Greasing should be left until the last minute, for two reasons. Firstly, you will avoid getting it on any of the tack, as you will have waited until the rider is up in the saddle and in control of the horse (i.e. you no longer have to touch the tack.) Secondly, the horse's body heat will eventually melt the grease. Use a pair of rubber gloves to make the job less messy; also you may have to lead the horse into the Start Box. If your hands – and therefore the reins – are covered in grease, it will make the rider's job of steering completely impossible.

Once the countdown has taken place and your rider is off on Phase D there is still plenty of work to be done. All the spare tack can now be put back into the trunk or bag. If you are going to wash the horse down when he comes back in from the Cross-Country you will have to refill the buckets, which may mean fetching water from the tanker. You will have about twelve to fourteen minutes to get everything tidied away and ready for the return of a very hot and tired horse.

It is permissible to lead excitable horses into the Starting Box. You can tell from this horse's expression that he knows exactly what will happen next!

In the Box after the Cross-Country

When they return, you will be completely involved with the horse and will not have time to see that all the equipment gets back to the stables. Delegate this job to one of your helpers and make it their responsibility to pack everything away and get it all safely back as soon as possible. Having

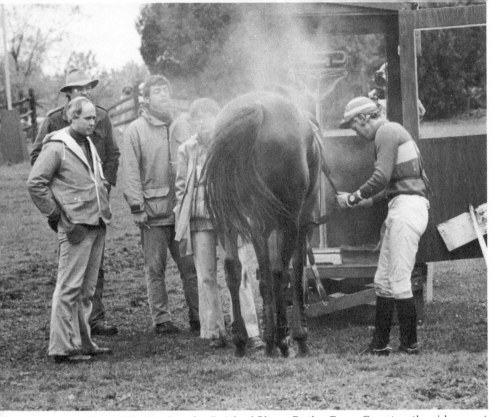

Immediately after the finish of Phase D, the Cross-Country, the rider must weigh-in. An official will hold the horse until this has been done. Note that here, in accordance with the rules, the rider is not being given help while unsaddling. Note, too, how hot and steamy the horse is. This is what a groom must be ready for.

organised this, go to the Finish with the headcollar and a towel – plus a sheet if necessary, depending on the weather.

As your rider finishes he will go up to the officials and ask permission to dismount. At this point no one is allowed to assist him in any way, and you should stand well back. The rider will then weigh-in, with or without the saddle, depending on whether or not he needs it to make up the weight. At this stage do not attempt to hold the horse or to help to take the saddle off; you must wait until the rider has weighed-in and the steward has confirmed that the weight is correct. If you do not obey the rules you could be responsible for eliminating your rider – which won't exactly make you the most popular person in town. So wait until the steward in charge of the scales tells you that you may take the horse.

Now you have a very tired and blowing horse on your hands. You have the choice of either cooling him down in the Box or of taking him straight back to the stables. We suggest that you cool him down in the Box. You have all your washing equipment ready and waiting and you can get to work straight away. Another advantage is that if the horse seems to be distressed there are vets on hand to advise you.

At many of the Events in the United States these days, you are not allowed to leave the Box area until your horse has recovered enough to indicate that all is well with him. We think that this is a very good idea. It is foolish to play 'Joe Vet' and it is comforting to know that the horse is somewhere where he can have the best possible care. The vets are more than willing to answer any of your questions and to double check the horse's vital signs. They are there to be made use of, so take advantage of their presence.

As your rider is unsaddling and weighing-in, you will have the opportunity to glance over the horse for any obvious signs of damage. If everything looks good, when you get the go-ahead you can take the bridle off – remembering to untie the bootlace – and put the headcollar on. Most horses that have just finished the Cross-Country will need to be walked for a few minutes before they can stand still long enough to be washed down. Therefore after you have stripped the tack off the horse it is a good idea to

Once the horse has partially recovered, the tack and boots are removed and the washing-down can begin. It is important to keep the hindquarters warm until the horse has completely cooled out and is back to normal. Then you can wash all the sweat away. If the horse is allowed to get cold before he has really recovered he may tie-up.

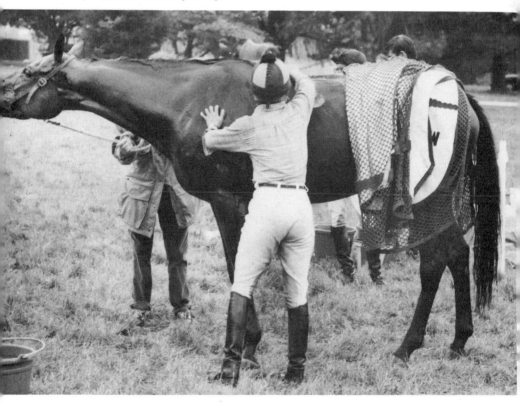

throw an anti-sweat sheet over his loins and quarters and lead him around for a few minutes. When he has caught his breath sufficiently to stand still for a while, hand him to your holder, and take off all the boots and bandages as quickly as you can. Check that there is no noticeable damage to the legs and then proceed to wash the horse down.

If it is very hot or if the horse seems to be over-heated, concentrate the iced water around the throat and neck and between his legs. Do not spill any water over the hind quarters until the horse has cooled out and the muscles have relaxed and have had time to cool down gradually on their own. Keep walking him for perhaps two minutes and then stop for thirty

If a horse finishes the Cross-Country extremely hot and with a high temperature, ice can be held between his hind legs and on his throat.

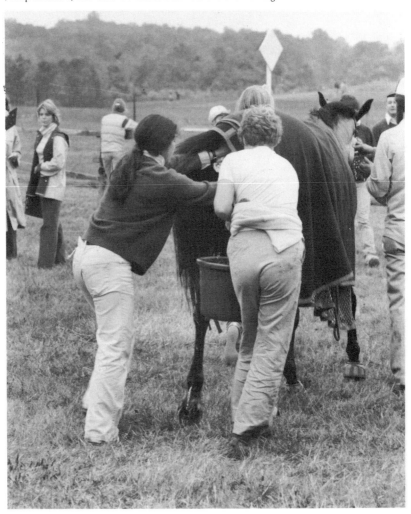

seconds to cool him down again with some more water. At this stage getting him clean is the last thing that should be on your mind; the most important objective is to cool him down to a point where his temperature, pulse, and respiration are normal. You *must* keep him walking. This will enable him to lose extra heat through convection and to prevent the muscles from seizing up. Of course, in colder weather you will probably not need ice, and your concern will lie in hitting the happy medium between washing the horse off and preventing him from catching cold.

Once you are happy that the horse is well on his way to full recovery you can put some sort of sheet on him and carry on walking him. At this point – let's say approximately twenty to thirty minutes after he has finished the Cross-Country – he can be offered something to drink, provided that he has stopped blowing. You can add electrolytes to the water, but this often puts a really thirsty horse off drinking. As he will invariably be somewhat dehydrated, the top priority must be to get some liquid into him. Allow him only four or five sips at a time. If you let him gulp down as much as he can – which at this point could be buckets – he will get a severe belly ache. Little and often should be the rule. Let him have a few sips, then walk him for a couple of minutes, then a few more sips, until he can be trusted not to bolt down an entire bucketful.

By now your team of helpers will have all the equipment packed and ready to go. Your rider will probably be telling the coach and the other riders how his round went, and your horse should have recovered sufficiently to be taken back to the stables. However, there are still a few things to do before you leave. First, ask the vet to double check that your horse is fit to leave (and do not forget to thank him). If your rider is planning to stay up at the Box until the end to help other riders, let him know that you are going back to the stables. He will probably want to check the horse's legs himself before you poultice them. Finally, it is a good idea to take out the studs before you move off. This will make life easier for the horse, especially if he will be walking on hard-topped roads on his way back to the stables. Bear in mind that there is always a chance that your horse may be drug tested at this point. If it happens, the officials concerned will generally allow you to see first to the horse's immediate needs.

At the Stables after the Speed and Endurance Test

Once back at the stables, put your horse in his stall – even if he still needs to walk a little more to cool down – so that he has the chance to stale and roll. This may seem unimportant, but it is necessary for the physical and mental comfort of the horse.

Unless there is some serious injury to attend to, keep walking the horse for as long as it takes to completely cool him out and until he is back to normal in all respects; this will probably take about an hour after he finishes Phase D. Keep offering him a few sips of water at a time. When his breathing is completely back to normal you can let him have something to eat. We prefer to let our horses have a little grass; 'Dr Green's' is the most natural feed and keeps the horses outside and moving about. At this stage you should be acutely aware of the horse's temperature; keep feeling under the sheet and make sure that he is neither too hot nor too cold.

It is now probably about an hour and a half after the finish. The horse has completely recovered, has had sufficient water to quench his thirst, and has picked at a little grass. If the weather is too bad for this, give him a small amount of hay. Your next job is to check him all over thoroughly for any scratches, bangs, heat or swellings. You need not wash him down again – at least, not his body. If you have used grease, you will probably have to wash the legs again before you can put on any poultice. Scrape off as much of the grease as you can and then use a detergent (making sure that it does not irritate the horse's skin) with plenty of warm water.

The use of whirlpool boots is one of the ways of reducing heat in a horse's legs after the rigours of the Cross-Country.

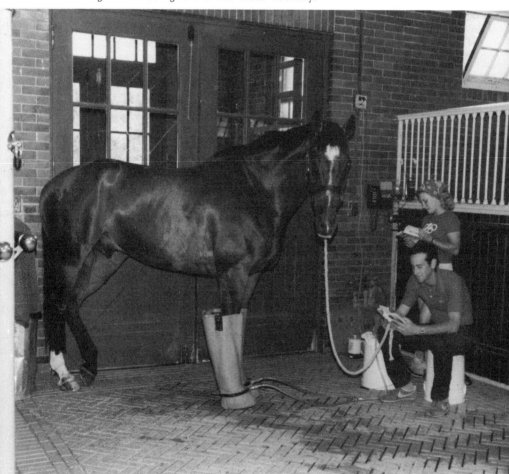

Never for a moment neglect your horse's well-being. He should not have to stand around for hours while you try to scrub all the grease off his legs. Do the best that you can within reason and without risking the horse's health.

Check his legs thoroughly, every inch of them. If there were hedges on the course, look for any thorns that may be lurking under the layer of hair. These can turn particularly nasty if they are missed and allowed to fester. Keep your eyes open for any cuts. If you find any, trim the surrounding hair away, so that you can see what you are dealing with, and treat each cut accordingly. Remember the illegal substances that you are not allowed to use. If you are in any doubt about any of your preparations, ask a vet.

After seeking out the obvious cuts and scratches, spend plenty of time checking the legs for heat, swellings and tenderness – all tell-tale signs of bruising or more serious tendon damage. At this stage in the game you should know your horse's legs like the back of your hand, so that even the tiniest blemish should tell you that something is wrong. A problem here is that because the horse is probably somewhat dehydrated it may be a day or two before any swelling will appear. So gentle, sensitive, hands must be methodically applied to the task of checking the legs.

Having checked all four legs thoroughly you can then cold-hose them – that is unless you are lucky enough to have a pair of 'whirlpool boots'. These are boots that are specially made for the horse's legs. You fill them with water – and even with crushed ice if you wish – then stand the horse in them for up to forty minutes while air is pumped into the boots. This causes the water to be in continual motion and is a good way of taking out the heat and the 'sting' from the legs after a long run on the cross-country course.

Whether or not you are fortunate enough to have these modern-day gadgets, you will now poultice the horse's legs. Again, how you do it is up to you. We advocate plastering all four legs thickly with poultice. Saturday night at a Three-Day Event is not the time to start skimping and saving on such a vital item as a poultice. Put it on from just below the knee, and try to have it high enough behind the knee so that it covers the check ligament. Then take it all the way down to well below the fetlock joint. Some people only poultice the back of the legs, covering the tendons only, but we believe that putting it all around the leg takes the sting out of the shins. The tendons are all in such close proximity to each other that instead of trying localised treatment it can only be of benefit to the horse if you cover the entire leg.

There are a number of materials that you can use to wrap a poultice. Among them are dampened newspaper, aluminium foil, and plastic wrap (cling film). They all have their advantages, so use whichever one suits you best, then cover with gamgee, and bandage.

Now your horse is nearly ready to be left alone for a while. Put some warm clothing on him, and if you plaited him, quickly take out the braids. Put him in his stall with some hay while you go and prepare a small mash for him. Using about two or three pounds of bran and one or two pounds of oats, make a mash well mixed with about one tablespoon of salt or

After a thorough check of the legs for any injury, poultice is applied thickly. This will soothe the legs and draw out any heat.

electrolytes. When the mash has cooled enough for eating, offer it to the horse. It may not seem much to give to an animal that has not eaten a square meal in probably twenty-four hours. However, that is just the point. You have to wean him back on to normal rations, and this must be done a little at a time. Be sure that the first food that goes through his stomach, apart from the small amount of grass or hay he may have had earlier, is easily digestible. This will prevent any impactions caused by too much dry feed in a stomach which is empty and which may be lacking in lubricants and digestive juices because of dehydration.

About forty minutes after the horse has eaten the mash you can offer him something more substantial, as long as he seems ready for it. By this time most horses are ready to eat the barn down, which is a good sign. From now on you can go back to your normal feeding routine. We hope that from all this you will see how a little precaution can be worth a ton of cure – and sometimes there is *no* cure for colic.

Now that your first priority, the horse, is happily munching away in his stable, all wrapped up in warm blankets and soothed by a poultice, with plenty of water and a square meal in front of him, you can slow down! In retrospect the last four hours will seem like a kaleidoscope of every activity in the book. Everything will have happened so quickly and there will have been so much to deal with. Yet whether you feel you are walking on air because everything went so well, or whether you are totally dejected because your team is at the bottom of the list, remember – as if you need to be reminded – there is still work to be done.

By this time all the gear from the Box will be back at the stables. You now have all the tack to clean and all the equipment to put away. This is really the worst job of the whole Event but the sooner it is done the sooner it will no longer be a problem. So before exhaustion finally catches up with you, attack it!

As you clean up the amazing amount of dirty tack that has accumulated, keep an eye on your horse without actually disturbing him. Take notice of how much or how little he is drinking and how interested he is in his hay and feed. If you suspect that anything is wrong, take his temperature, check that he has not broken-out and, if you feel you need assistance, ask the vet to take a look at him.

At the end of the day, when all the competitors have finished riding and all the clearing up has been done, your rider and coach will most likely want to see your horse walk and trot out to see how stiff he is – or there may be a soundness problem that has manifested itself in the last few hours. Some horses may be perfectly sound at the time that they finish the course, but after a while, when the adrenalin has stopped flowing and the stiffness has set in, they can suddenly look very lame. *Most* horses will show stiffness to some degree at this point in the proceedings, and it is up to your rider and the team coach or Chef d'Equipe to decide how to go about making the horse supple enough for the next day. By knowing your horse – because you have had your finger on his 'pulse' for the past six months or more – you will have a very good idea of the extent of the stiffness or injury. Some horses always come out looking as though they cannot move

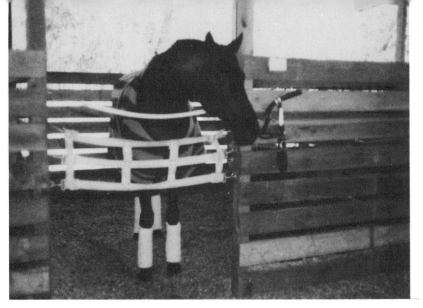

After the Speed and Endurance the horse is comfortably rugged, bandaged, bedded and sufficiently recovered to be looking with interest over the stall guards.

– then, miraculously, walk out of it in a few minutes. Others, who are normally tough and who have only a slight stiffness, could be showing signs of something more serious. So you can see how important it is to know your individual horse. The rider, too, will know if there were any moments on the course when the horse may have over-exerted himself, or may have banged a leg on a fence. There are really no set rules as to how a horse should look after the Cross-Country.

If there is an obvious point of bruising, hosing can do much to bring down the swelling – and walking and massaging will often do wonders for stiff and tired horses. The aim is to help your horse to the utmost without depriving him of his rest; he will need as much as he can get, and any treatment must be balanced against this. Though we agree that walking a stiff horse can help tremendously, we do not see the point in walking non-stop all night.

This first trot-up after the Cross-Country will probably take place at, say, five or six in the evening. If the horse is free of any treatable injuries, and seems all right or just a little stiff, hand walk him for about half an hour and allow him to pick at some grass. But you must make sure that he is warm at all times – this is most important at this stage. Just like a human being, a horse will feel the cold more easily when he is tired, and if you do not keep him warm enough you are just inviting more stiff muscles and joints. In fact it can be beneficial to massage the horse all over with a rub to keep the muscles warm and relaxed. Most important of all, keep a very close eye on his temperature and make sure that there are no draughts in his stall. You can then put him away with some more hay and perhaps a little feed.

Now it is your turn to relax! Have a soothing bath and eat some substantial food. There are often parties on Cross-Country night, but these should be resisted until after you have made a final check on your horse, sometime between ten and eleven o'clock. When you go back to the stables for this final check, wait for your rider and coach before you take the horse out of the stall. The first few steps are a good indication of how he is feeling. Do not remove the bandages – this can be done in the morning. When everyone has arrived, take the horse out and start by walking up and down, preferably on a well-lit, flat surface, enabling the horse to see where he is going. Take your time, and allow him to have his head, so that your rider can see exactly how the horse is feeling. If the weather is warm enough, remove all the rugs. If not, make sure that the front of the rug is not binding tightly across the horse's chest and shoulders, which could make a tired and sore horse trot up unevenly. Then you can trot up and down. Often the first few steps may be very shaky, then as the stiffness wears off the rhythm and soundness will return. What you are seeing now is a fair indication of the sort of animal that you will have in the morning. Now that 'bute' (phenylbutazone) is illegal at many competitions, and there is therefore no way of chemically disguising any unsoundness, you will have to resort to the old methods such as walking, massaging, hosing, and poulticing. There are also many electrical gadgets which act on the muscles and work out any adhesions or stiffnesses; these are good but need to be operated by someone who knows what they are doing.

We would say that in our experience the majority of animals at this stage of the Event look their worst. They are almost invariably very tired and, to some extent, stiff – which is understandable. You will therefore probably be walking your horse in an attempt to ward off onward-creeping stiffnesses. Up to one hour's walking is about the optimum amount of time you need to loosen up a very stiff horse. If after this there is no improvement, something must be seriously wrong, and how to deal with it must be a decision for your rider, the coach and the vet.

At the World Championships in Germany in 1982, five sets of deep-heat lamps were made available to us, with a very helpful man who told us how to use them on our horses to alleviate stiffness. They proved invaluable, as we alternated half an hour of deep-heat lamp treatment with half an hour of walking, then half an hour of rest. This was done twice with *The Saint*, on Saturday night and then repeated on the Sunday morning, so that we were able to turn a very stiff horse into a very supple and ready-to-run athlete.

Once the final look at the horse has taken place and you have walked him for a little while longer, put him away with, perhaps, a final meal. Double check that he is warm enough, take his temperature, then say good-night and either head for bed or, if you have found some energy from somewhere, go off to that party – you've earned it!

A brief postscript to this chapter. If you have more than one horse to look after you must have enough people to help you. Should anything serious happen to the first horse you must have someone capable of either staying with him or of relieving you in the Box so that you can attend to him. As the number of horses in your care grows, so you will have to increase the number of helpers and the amount of planning.

CHAPTER NINE

The Three-Day Event: Show Jumping

The last morning of the competition will find any groom worth her salt out and about at some ridiculously early hour. The first official happening is the *Third Veterinary Inspection*. This is nearly always scheduled for early on in the day, somewhere between nine o'clock and twelve noon, and your horse will have to be turned out immaculately, leaving little time for you to do anything else but concentrate on him.

If the trot-up late the previous night showed the horse to be sound, though a little stiff, you will most probably have to spend only half to one hour on loosening and limbering him up. If the problem is worse, and your rider or team still plan to run him, you must expect to be alert and ready at crack of dawn.

Let us suppose that the inspection is at nine, and you know that your horse is stiff but should loosen up after an hour's hand walk. Plan on getting to the stables at five-thirty am. Most riders will want to see the horse jog up, so do not take the horse out until the rider arrives. Feed and water him – checking that nothing untoward has happened during the night – and muck-out while he is eating. Take the bandages off and as much of the poultice as you can, without disturbing the horse. Check that the legs are no more swollen now than they were yesterday, and feel for any spots that are noticeably warmer. Check the feet for heat, too, as on hard or rocky terrain a horse that is not wearing pads under his shoes can suffer a stone bruise.

As soon as the rider arrives, take the horse out and walk him up and down a couple of times to see exactly how stiff he is, and to give him the chance to loosen up a little before asking him to trot. Then trot him up two or three times; you will often find that a horse who looks as if he can hardly bring himself to move on the first trot will be perfectly all right by the third or fourth.

After this private examination by yourselves, wash off all the remaining poultice and double check the legs again. If you notice anything, however small, do not hesitate to point it out to your rider. Any slight warmth, swelling, or tenderness is often an indication of something going on inside the legs.

Your number one priority now is to get your horse supple and sound enough to be able to pass the inspection that will be held by the panel of judges and vets. Grooming him and removing the remainder of the grease is secondary at this moment. Do whatever your rider or coach has decided must be done. It may be a hand walk, or the rider may decide to take the horse out for a long, slow limbering hack. Whatever it is, it should be done straight away, so that there is no last-minute rush to warm him up because you have been plaiting and polishing.

By now it is about six thirty am. If it has been decided to give the horse a forty-minute hand walk, set off with him at once. Remember that the point of this exercise is to walk so that the horse loosens up and gets the stiffness out of the muscles. It is not supposed to be a social occasion for *you*. Many times on a Jumping Day morning we have seen grooms who were supposed to be walking their horses, but who instead had their heads locked together in some deeply riveting gossip while the horse waited about, standing in the early morning chill – certainly not stretching any muscles and, if anything, just feeling the cold. A hand walk means *walk*. Of course, it is fine to let him pick at the grass now and then – but get those muscles working. Make sure at all times that your horse is warm enough; he will be feeling the cold more easily now that he is tired, especially if you have clipped him.

This will bring you up to about seven o'clock. Put the horse away for a while, to pick at some hay and stale, while you gather together everything that you will need. First, collect the bridle – although it is quite permissible to jog a horse up at an inspection in a headcollar. He may have a sore mouth or he may just jog better in a headcollar than in a bridle. Have the bridle numbers ready if needed – or the number for the person jogging the horse to wear around the waist or arm.

Next you must remove any grease that may still be stuck to the horse, and you will soon discover what a nuisance this can be! Hot water, some sort of detergent and plenty of patience, are what are needed. Do not spend too much time doing this, as you are likely to make the horse's legs sore with all that rubbing. You will probably still be finding traces of grease a week later. An excellent waterless grease-remover is 'Swarfega', normally used by mechanics. Or instead of using Vaseline you could have used a greaseless 'bag balm', which is almost as effective but far easier to remove.

Next we come to the question of plaiting. There are two schools of thought here. If you plait for the veterinary inspection, not only will the horse look smartly turned out, but he will already be plaited for the Show Jumping later on in the day. This means that although you will be fiddling around the horse most of the morning, once he is plaited and has passed the inspection he will be allowed to rest until the parade before the Jumping. On the other hand, some people feel that as long as the horse has a neatly pulled mane it is better to let him rest rather than suffer the hour-long hairdressing session that will be needed. Also, should your horse fail to pass (failing to pass one of these examinations or inspections is called being 'spun'), you will not have plaited him up in vain. At some Events there is more time after the inspection and before the Jumping to plait up if necessary. Once again, it is up to you, your rider, or your coach. In a team event the choice will be made for you, as it will be a team rule that the horses are all plaited or are all 'au naturel'.

By seven-thirty any washing and grooming should have been done, especially if you are going to plait, which should take you until just after eight o'clock. Then, depending on where your horse is in the order of inspection, tack him up, put on a good day rug, then take him out and lead him around for about half an hour before you are called to jog.

It is essential to practice jogging the horse before you go in. You may, for example need help in reminding the horse to move away freely and not to drag behind. If you are to jog the horse yourself, make sure that you are tidy and presentable. It would be a shame if having spent a long time in polishing up your horse you were the one who looked like a disaster area.

The Third Inspection is just like the First Inspection, in that the Jury are looking for marked lameness or poor general condition, and they have full power to eliminate any horse found unfit for competition. Once it is over, take your horse back to the stables for a rest and an early lunch.

Collect a time schedule from the stable manager. This will tell you which horses are still in the competition, and in what order they will be jumping. It will also give the time of the parade and the time by which everyone is expected to be at the arena. Consult with your rider when he would like the horse to be ready. Obviously, if your horse is going to be one of the first to jump, it would be a good idea to arrange it so that the rider can warm-up before the parade, thus avoiding a last-minute rush.

As the Show Jumping is the finale of the Three-Day Event, you will have to be thinking about packing up and planning your return home. The Jumping is usually held in the early afternoon and is preceded by a parade of all the competitors. Should you find that the timetable allows a couple of free hours you would do well to utilize them by packing up all the equipment you will not be needing again. Also, if you are driving off that night make sure that you have enough fuel to get you home; a small point but it is not very easy to find gas (petrol) or diesel late on a Sunday night.

Have all your tack ready for the Show Jumping. Under the new FEI Rules it is no longer necessary for the rider to carry a minimum required weight in this final phase, so you do not have to worry about lead and weight pads. If you are part of a team, sew the flag-cloth on to the saddle pad. Have the correct numbers for the horse's bridle, if they are required. Your last job before tacking-up will be to put the studs in. If you whipped them out quickly yesterday in the Box without packing the stud holes, allow a little extra time for this.

Usually the Show Jumping area is not within easy walking distance, and you can bet your boots that the whole performance will be a long drawn-out affair. First there is the parade of competitors, then the actual competition and finally the prize-giving. You can safely say that you and your horse will probably be up there for at least three hours. If this is the case, ask for permission to bring your trailer or horse box up to the Show Jumping area. You can then put your horse away for a while in between displays, so that he does not have to hang about, especially if it is cold or raining.

If you don't have the luxury of the horse box or trailer, you will have to go up to the arena with enough blankets to cope with all sorts of weather. If you take only a fly sheet you can guarantee that it will rain cats and dogs. So take a bucket and brush, a rub rag, some fly spray, and an assortment of studs and sheets. Do not forget the headcollar, and a waterproof coat for yourself. Another suggestion: even if your rider does not want the horse to wear boots in the actual competition it is a wise move to put them on for the parade and for the prize-giving. This is just one more precaution against

All the equipment that is needed at the Show Jumping collecting ring: rugs, headcollars, grooming accessories and the rider's clothes.

possible injury. It is so easy for horses to get over-excited in the parade, and then to become very difficult to control; they often ricochet about the arena, oblivious to the presence of other animals, and can easily kick or step on *your* unsuspecting horse (which, of course, is behaving impeccably). This fracas can also happen in the excitement of the victory gallop and it would be a shame for your horse to sustain an injury at the final stage of the Event, particularly an injury that could easily have been prevented.

You must not lose sight of what your job is today. It is very easy to become carried away on a wave of elation if your horse or team look to be in with a winning chance; it is equally easy to become despondent and lax if your horse is so far down the list that it seems pointless to stay around.

The warm-up area on Show Jumping day is generally something of a bear garden, and the groom's presence is essential to the rider's well-being.

Whatever the chances and whatever the outcome, your job is to look after the horse, and you are not being true to yourself if you do not make every effort to care for him. He will be, at best, just slightly tired and, at worst, very tired and stiff. You have to make him as comfortable as you can in the circumstances, and this means keeping him warm, supple, and calm. Do not forget the tension that is part and parcel of occupying a top placing: your rider's nerves may be stretched to the limit with this responsibility. Treat today's happenings with a calm and philosophical attitude; it will all be over sooner than you could believe.

Once you are up at the Jumping arena, be within easy sight and sound of your rider all the time. It would be nice to be able to watch all the rides, but your rider may need assistance at any time – calling for another blanket, or some more fly spray. Before you even leave the stable area, discuss with your rider what his warming-up plans will be. This will give you some idea of the type of fences he will require, once he starts to warm-up the horse.

After the parade, if there is a long gap until your rider needs to get mounted, and you do not have your trailer within easy reach, loosen the girth and noseband and throw an appropriate sheet over the horse to keep him warm. In hotter places, instead of keeping the horse warm, you will need a fly sheet and, if you can find it, an area that affords some shade from the sun. If it is cold, keep the horse walking for a while, then rest in a sheltered spot well away from the confusion that often prevails in and around the practice area. Some horses find the noise of the loud-speakers and the sudden applause of the crowd upsetting. However, with calm and sensible handling on your part he should soon get used to it. Just stay calm and reassure him, and do not go into areas that are overflowing with people and that have three speakers overhead. If you do, you will not be the only one to get hurt!

The Jumping phase is different from any other, basically because you are dealing with animals tired after the gruelling demands of the Cross-Country. Therefore the warming-up exercises should be gradual and well thought out, stretching the horse a little more each time until he can comfortably jump without stress or strain. Your rider will probably spend quite a while doing limbering-up exercises with the horse on the flat; trotting and cantering, lengthening and shortening – all different routines aimed at getting the horse supple and responsive and ready to jump fences.

You probably do not need to be told how dangerous practice arenas can be to your health! Horses will be coming in all directions, and all of them fighting for a chance to jump one of the three fences. Everyone agrees that there should be more practice fences but, unfortunately, the space or the spare fences are not always available. Often it would be helpful to the riders if a simple grid was provided, but this may be asking too much. All you can hope for is a vertical, an oxer or parallel and, ideally, a smaller fence, such as a two-foot cross rail that can stay at that height throughout, so there is always something small for the riders to begin with. This helps everyone and does away with the need to be continually dismantling the vertical and therefore invariably upsetting someone.

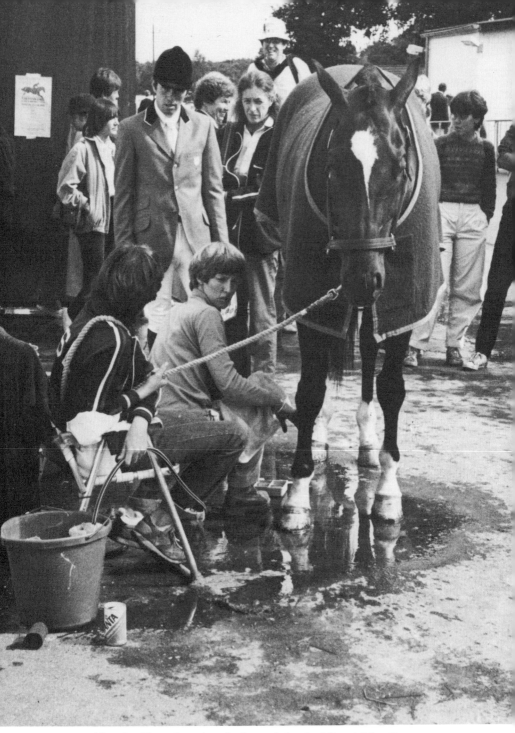

After the Show Jumping the horse is back at the stables; the grooms are taking out studs and preparing to cold-hose while the anxious rider waits to make sure that all is well.

Remember that the practice fences are flagged in the same way as the competition fences – that is, they must be jumped with a red flag on the right and a white flag on the left. Failure to jump a practice fence in the correct direction may lead to elimination. Be aware of this when you build the fences, and be ready to warn any forgetful rider who is headed the wrong way. This rule is for everyone's safety and should prevent any chance of a mid-air collision. While you are working around the fences keep your eyes and ears peeled for approaching horses and do not forget that your rider is not the only one trying to warm up. If there is someone who is jumping before your rider, let him have first use of the fence. It is all a matter of common sense and common courtesy.

Keep a programme on you at all times and know who is drawn to go just before your rider. After your rider has warmed up he will probably stay on the horse to keep him moving, and will need to make sure he knows when his turn is approaching. Sometimes the rider may decide to get off and watch, and will give you the horse to lead around. Do not go too far away and do not let the horse graze until after he has finished his round. Keep an ear open in case the steward calls your horse to the collecting area, and be ready to slip off the headcollar and sheet and throw your rider into the saddle.

Should you be helping your rider to warm-up, and you are the one whose opinion he asks as to how the horse is jumping – be constructive. Time is very short and you have to take into account the fitness of the horse; you cannot expect him to be jumping exuberantly over the fences when he would probably prefer to be left in a cosy stable with a big manger of feed. Be practical. You should, by now, know what your rider expects – and also the horse's own particular style. If it appears that the horse is trying his best, even though he would never make it as an open jumper with such a performance, praise him. Remember that nerves will be fairly tattered by now, and that any derogatory remark is really not going to improve the situation. Sometimes building big or tricky fences will encourage a horse to try that little bit harder. However, this is up to the rider or the coach, so do not attempt to do anything without consent. Just give psychological support to your rider – and be cheerful.

Once rider and horse have entered the ring, there is nothing left for you to do but hold your breath. Three-Day Eventing can certainly add the grey hairs and wrinkles faster than anything else we know!

With any luck, the round will have been clear; if not, at least you know that all concerned have tried their hardest but were just beaten on the day. It happens to the best. Whether you are up in seventh heaven or down in the pits, remember why you are doing this. It is because you enjoy it and because most of the time it is fun. You are adult enough to understand what good sportsmanship is, and if it has been someone else's turn to collect the laurels you should genuinely be able to share in their excitement and happiness. After all, you have all been tested by the same course, rather than by each other!

Your job is still not quite finished! When your rider has come out of the arena and dismounted you can then take the horse, loosen the noseband

and girth, and throw a sheet of some sort over him. He may be hot, so a few minutes walking around will be in order. There are two things to note here. The next happening will be the prize-giving, so get the horse ready by putting on the boots, which we mentioned earlier. And there is still the possibility of your horse being chosen for a random dope test, so be prepared for it.

During the prize-giving ceremony you will no doubt experience all sorts of emotions – but there still isn't time for daydreaming. Once the horse is out of the arena there's more work to be done. You must now loosen his girth and noseband, return his numbers if you have to, make sure that he is warm enough, and take him on back to the stables. Put him in his stall, untack him and take out his studs. Leave him in peace for five minutes so that he can roll and stale if he wishes. Ration the water if he is very thirsty, and give him some hay. All he will probably want to do is eat and rest, so carry out what you have to in the way of making him comfortable as quickly as you can. Take out his plaits, sponge over his saddle patch if necessary, but do not spend a long time washing him down at this point. A little bit of dirt is not going to harm him, and having you fussing around him will not be appreciated. Wrap his legs up warmly for the time being, even if you plan on poulticing him again later. Put on some suitable blankets, make him up a mash with lots of goodies, such as apples and carrots, and leave him in peace for a while.

The end of the Event. Rider, groom and helper load up the box.

Job satisfaction..The groom has won a trophy, as well as the rider.

Now you can either be an exemplary groom and clean all the tack that has just arrived from the jumping arena, or you can go off and get yourself a well-earned drink. Even if you do not want to imbibe, this may be the last chance you have of seeing everyone before they all pack up and head for home. The fact that there are such nice people in this sport is one of the main reasons why you are in it. You will meet all sorts of characters and hundreds of big warm hearts, so if you have the chance to relax at the end of the competition with all your friends – albeit just for a short while – do it. More grooms should realise that there is more to a Three-Day Event than the inside of a stable and a tack cleaning bucket. Unless it is absolutely necessary to leave that evening, it is better for the horse to have a decent night's rest before travelling home. It is also more practical for you, too, as only the strongest people feel up to a long drive after a weekend such as this one will have been. So, all being well, the packing and cleaning up can be left until tomorrow.

Later, after the drinks and the farewells, and after the horse has had a rest and something to eat, take him out for a leg stretch and a bite of grass. Now you can poultice him again if you want to. This is a good idea, as it will take away any aches that may have occurred as a result of the Show Jumping. Also, there will still be concussion and soreness in the legs from the Cross-Country.

Keep a close eye on your horse. He may show signs of fatigue, but any change in temperature must also be recorded. Having taken his temperature, if you are not satisfied that he is feeling all right, consult a vet. Should a very tired animal not be allowed to rest and be made to travel immediately after such an Event, there could be problems, and you may end up with a very sick horse indeed. So at this stage awareness of his well-being is of utmost importance. He will need to stock up on fluids, so keep a constant supply of clean water available at all times and be aware of how much or how little he is drinking. If the weather has been very hot or he seems dehydrated, add electrolytes or salt to his feed. Although he will have missed out on a few feedings, gradually cut back on his protein intake, as he will be doing nothing for a while and you will want to avoid his tieing-up.

After you have looked after the horse, cleaned your gear and packed it away, go and find the stable manager and thank him. All stable managers are worth their weight in gold. Most of them are volunteers (goodness knows why they do it!) and they do a tremendous job, sorting out and putting up with all our own individual needs. So they deserve your hearty thanks. You can also show your gratitude in a practical way – by making sure that your area is as clean and tidy as you found it. Why should someone else have to come and clear up after you? If everyone left without tidying up there would be enough work for an army. Be thoughtful, and you may be asked back again. Maybe one day you will end up as stable manager at an Event – and then you will need all the help you can get.

CHAPTER TEN

The Aftermath

So you, your horse and your rider have completed a Three-Day Event. You are all feeling pretty tired, but through luck and good judgement you have come out of it unscathed. There is always a feeling of sadness as you leave the site of a Three-Day Event: you are saying goodbye to a place that holds a lot of memories for all concerned. Although you will only have been here for a week or so, it will seem more like a year.

What next? Long-term plans at this point will be sketchy. If your horse has performed satisfactorily, you may be looking forward to bigger and better things for next season. If the result was not as good as you had hoped for, perhaps the horse will have to climb down a rung or two and start the new season on a slightly less demanding level until he has mastered his task a little better.

Conveniently, most Three-Day Events are scheduled at the end of a season. Therefore all of you – especially the horse – will have at least a month or two when you can take a well-earned break from the pressures and whirlwind pace. Competition is so fierce and training so demanding that a complete rest is essential for the horse, particularly a young one. It is not only a time in which the horse's body can recuperate and strengthen, but also in which he can mentally unwind, relax and be refreshed before the next season.

Let us now concentrate on your arrival back home immediately after a Three-Day Event, and go step-by-step into the holiday season. Although you will probably feel like falling into bed for a week, it is vital that you now keep just as close an eye on your horse as ever before. The next three or four days are very important to his well-being. He will be feeling at his lowest ebb, and it is at this time when any damage that did not show up before will probably become visible. At the Event, the horse will have been living, as you will have been, on the adrenalin, stimulated by all the excitement. Once he is at home, in familiar and relaxed surroundings, all the aches and pains will suddenly become obvious. Not only will he feel the extent of his aches and tiredness but – after he has had plenty of time to recover any lost body fluids – bruises and swellings are likely to appear. Should you have been competing in an Event in which you were allowed to administer 'bute', it will have worn away and all the fillings it prevented will appear.

What do you do with a tired horse heading for a rest? You cannot just throw him out into a field and forget about him until the next season. As with anything else to do with horses, a gradual process has to be the rule of thumb.

The majority of horses will have been turned out for only about one or two hours a day at the most during their build-up to a Three-Day Event, so turning them out now has to be done gradually. A horse is still stiff at this point. If he is just thrown out into a field, the stiffness may become permanent. So for the first week after an Event it is advisable to keep him in some sort of light work, to prevent any adhesions from forming. This can be achieved either by frequent hand walks or by light hacks of up to an hour: nothing terribly demanding: you know how stiff you yourself feel if you do not exercise after you have done something particularly strenuous. As long as the horse has suffered no hurt that will be made worse by light exercise, keep him up for about a week, alternating hacking or hand walks with periods of turn-out. Gradually the time spent out in the field can be lengthened until he may be happily left out all day. There is always an exception to every rule, and sometimes you will find horses that do poorly when they are completely let down and turned out. Also, older horses may be better if they stay in light work, because physically they need to be kept in some sort of shape. This will prevent stiffness taking over their bodies to such an extent that when they are brought back into work they are so stiff and crocketty that it feels almost cruel to ride them. Much will depend on the facilities available. You may not have the facilities or the grass to enable you to turn your horse out all day. Other than finding some kind friends to let you use their fields, you are better off keeping the horse in very light work.

When you do turn out, make sure that the horse is warm enough and that his legs are well protected. A companion pony may be necessary to prevent this ultra-fit athlete from galloping around like a maniac.

Because of his change in work you should modify his feed-chart, cutting down on the proteins and increasing the bulk and fattening food stuffs, such as boiled feeds and hay. This is a very individual matter, and the older the horse the less likely you will be to cut down on the protein: in fact, maize is a very good foodstuff for older horses, but it is very high in protein. So be aware of what your horse is eating and feed him according to his needs, both physical and mental. A highly fit horse that has been on a high-protein diet is prone to tieing-up if his feeding programme is not carefully monitored and tailored to his own special needs.

Our experience has shown us that horses look their skinniest on the third or fourth day after an Event. Be ready for this and try to catch it before the horse loses so much condition that you end up spending the whole holiday time trying to put all the lost weight back on. With this possibility in mind, do not be too eager to cut back his feed too soon.

Another sign to watch for and to interpret is one of boredom. Like human beings who have been highly active and then abruptly halted, horses find it difficult to relax and to just plain enjoy doing nothing. It may take a horse a week or two to appreciate freedom from work and routine. Often they will stay out in the paddock for only a few minutes before they are back at the gate, asking to come in. Try just ignoring it, and after a few days they should get the message. If this fails, continue to hack out quietly every day until you reach a point where the horse is let down enough mentally to be able to stay out. If this does not work, and giving him companions to play with is just as useless, you may find that you will have to keep him in light work throughout the off season.

Though we would not advise riding without a hard hat, standing a horse in the sea or stream to cool his legs is a recommended part of the letting-down programme. Note the rugs for warmth.

Of course all this will depend largely on the quality of the grass available, because few horses will ignore a lush pasture in preference to work! Another reason why we think it is so beneficial to turn horses out is that, as mentioned before, we are great believers in the power of 'Dr Green' – good old grass. If you have ample grazing, especially at the end of the spring season, it is great if you can wean your horse off hard feed completely and just let him get his keep from the grass. This is the most natural and best form of food for him, as long as there is enough and he looks to be doing well on it. It will clean out his system and give his insides the chance to relax and have a vacation from all the oats and additives that have been going through him in the past months.

A few other points to think of now at this time are shoeing, worming, and teeth. If the ground is soft enough, it is often good for your horse to go without shoes. This has many advantages. First of all it will encourage horses with small, and even constricted feet to spread and grow. It will also mean that if you are turning him out with others you will not have the worry of their hurting each other should they be playing with their shoes

Happiness is taking the weight off your legs.

on. When the shoes are first removed and the horse has to go barefoot you will see him moving about a little gingerly to begin with, just as you would on a rocky beach. This is good, in that it will prevent the horse from galloping around and perhaps hurting himself in some way during the first few days of freedom after not being turned out for some time. Even though he may not have shoes, you must keep his feet in good condition by having the blacksmith trim them every four or five weeks. To ignore the feet until the next season is a completely false economy, and sadly something that happens all too often. Now is the time to work on them, especially if they are constricted and need encouragement to spread. Similarly, if they are flat and dished they should not be allowed to get out of hand. By allowing the horse to go barefoot you will increase the circulation and this will often mean that the feet will grow more rapidly than before.

Once the horse has recovered from the initial fatigue and is well on his way to putting on some weight and unwinding in the field, you can ask your vet to attend to a couple of items. One is a blood count, to see if everything is fine inside him, and the other is a worm count. It would be silly not to have these things done now. If you find that your horse is slightly anaemic – which is often the case after a Three-Day Event – you can treat it right away with vitamins, rather than letting it get worse and thus allowing the horse's condition to drop away instead of improving.

All in all, your horse is as important in rest as he is in work. Though the pressure is off you to some extent, it is still your job to look after the horse to the best of your ability, to understand what all his little mannerisms mean, and to catch something that is not just quite right before it becomes a problem. After an Event you have to be as vigilant as ever, trotting the horse up every day to ensure that he is still sound. Watch for anything that may not be normal, and do not dismiss something that you cannot completely explain. The most important things to do when you are at home after an Event are to watch his soundness, his weight, and his warmth. Keeping a day-by-day régime and a knowledge of the horse's individual needs as your guidelines, you cannot go far wrong in the care of your horse after a big competition.

CHAPTER ELEVEN

Standing Back, Looking Forward

So, there you are. We hope that you now have enough tips under your belt to understand and handle a Three-Day Event a little better. Whether you are a groom, parent, friend, owner, or trainer, there is so much you can do to make the Event run a little smoother for the horse and rider. Being part of a team – whether at a Pony Club Rally or an Olympic Games – is what it's all about, and every member of the team has to be strong. It can be a most rewarding experience for all those taking part.

There's nothing to beat the exhilarating feeling that comes with winning a medal. Yet there is almost a similar feeling of elation, mixed with relief, when your horse has missed the golden disc but has gone *so* well, and tried *so* hard. All that really matters is that he is home safe and sound.

In looking after a competition horse there is so much to be gained and learned and if, like us, you have been fortunate enough to work for good employers and to travel abroad, the experience can be very gratifying.

Grooming full-time for a top-class Event stable is extremely tiring, both physically and mentally. The higher the goal, the higher the risk, and along with the gains there are also many heartaches and disappointments. In contrast with other jobs, you are dealing with an animal, whom you spend many hours caring for and who because he is a competition horse is sometimes asked to perform beyond his maximum capabilities, and the outcome may not always be satisfactory.

Let's give an example. Picture an Event yard where months have been spent training and caring for a horse in preparation for an International Three-Day Event. Not only will the horse and rider be competing against the best in the world, but they have the additional responsibility of representing their country. Imagine the excitement, the hopes and the dreams!

Dressage day goes well; but now comes the moment of truth. You have led the horse to the start of the Cross-Country, and he and his rider are off on the most challenging and difficult phase of the competition. All you can do now is to wait anxiously in the Box and listen to the commentary.

When horse and rider gallop through the finish flags, you are filled with relief and delight. However, you learn that another combination in your Team could not tackle the enormous course and had to retire half-way round. That leaves the minimum number of three Team members for the Show Jumping the next day. (Although there are four riders in each Team, only the scores of the top three are counted, so your Team is still in the running.) The score board tells the rider that his Team is in the lead, and that they only have to complete the Show Jumping satisfactorily to win the Gold Medal.

The rider comes back to the stable to relay the good news, only to find his groom worried because the horse has an injury which may be bad enough to prevent him from competing the next day. The vet, the coach, the rider, the groom, all gather round. A decision has to be made. There is a great deal at stake for everyone, including the horse. Is he to run and possibly damage himself irreparably so that his Eventing career is finished? Or should the medal be forfeited and the horse withdrawn so that with proper rest and care he may compete next season? There is a Team to be considered, and the chance of a lifetime is in the balance.

This is a moment when there may be conflicting opinions – and it may be hard for you to withhold your own personal emotions. Your sole aim and responsibility over the past years has been the care and well-being of the horse with whom you have developed a very special rapport, but you know that the final decision is not, in fact, yours. Now *you* are being put to the test, and you must have the discipline and courage to carry on even if you don't agree with the decision.

Fortunately, situations such as these don't often arise, but they *can* happen once in a while, and they are very difficult to solve in a way acceptable to everyone. Though most Event grooms are respected by their riders, and their opinion is often sought when decisions of any magnitude are being made, you can't take this for granted.

Now let's get back to the theme of this chapter. As the sport is expanding rapidly throughout the world, the groom's job is becoming more and more professional and specialised. At the start of a grooming career, there's so much to absorb that the first few years will flash by. As anyone involved with horses knows, there is always something new to learn, to observe, to master. As you become more confident and capable, you may be lucky enough to travel, especially abroad. You should take full advantage of every opportunity to acquire new and possibly better techniques of horse-care by studying how Event horses in other countries are looked after. You can go on extending your knowledge, thus keeping the job continually interesting and progressive. Not to mention the fact that wherever you go, you will meet interesting people, make new friends, and widen your horizons.

After a few years, however, there may come a time when you feel you

What it is all about.

must stand back and take a good long look at where you are and where you are going in your career. There are numerous possibilities: for instance, many grooms are now freelancing. A rider may be able to manage perfectly well on his own at home but will need experienced help at an Event.

You could, on the other hand, start your own yard and be manager over other grooms. Or your equestrian background might be of help in working for a tack store or a firm that manufactures or sells horse equipment.

There are also many grooms who have moved on to teaching, or, depending on their riding ability, to riding for a stable. And if you have been lucky enough to travel overseas, you may have made useful contacts that open other doors. But think hard before you make a change. Be as sure as you can that it's going to be a change for the better.

Whatever job you decide on, find out the terms and conditions first – salary, accommodation, time off and holidays, duties and responsibility, and, most important, insurance policies. Because you are dealing with horses, accidents can happen, and you must make sure that you are properly insured against injuries. You must definitely have a written contract which covers these points; this is only fair to both parties.

Eventing is known for its friendliness and sportsmanship as well as for its incredibly high standards. As long as everyone involved in the sport that we love so dearly remembers what attracted them to it in the first place – the horse, the excitement, and the fun – then we believe that all will be well for the future. Good, conscientious grooms will be drawn to the sport, and older grooms will be encouraged to stay a little longer, or perhaps branch out into other aspects of Eventing. But always remember that you must gain your experience step by step, and be aware that miracles don't happen overnight.

If you are given the chance to do your job in an atmosphere conducive to learning, you in turn must appreciate what you are entering into, and must give your best.

Whatever your personal reasons for your interest in Eventing, as long as the horse is never made to suffer through your negligence or ambition, you will be contributing to the welfare of the sport, and if the sport continues to grow and flourish, so will the rôle of the groom.

Additional Notes on Health and Injuries

Looking back through this book there are a few items in the category of health and injuries which are mentioned several times. As they are of some importance, we thought it would be helpful to expand on them. The notes which follow are based on our own research and personal experience.

Colic

Colic is the name generally given to any sort of abdominal pain. There are many different kinds, varying from a mild, easily remedied colic, to the (sometimes) fatal, twisted-gut type. Most of them are caused by poor management. Things to avoid are: too much 'concentrated' feed, especially when fed too soon before or after hard work; poor quality feed; mouldy hay; boiled grains that have only been partially cooked; the drinking of large quantities of water while hot and sweaty; grazing on lush young pasture, especially if the horse has been stabled for any length of time; poisonous plants, or foreign bodies such as sand or string, that can enter the horse's system through grazing or feedstuffs; an infestation of worms, which can cause irreparable internal damage. Also, impactions due to lack of fluid intake are common both in the heat of summer and in the cold of winter, when iced-over buckets or frozen water restrict normal consumption.

The symptoms of colic vary in severity, but most horses indicate abdominal discomfort by rolling, sweating, looking and kicking at their stomach, and pawing the ground. They will also go off their food and there may be an increase in their respiration. In severe cases there will also be a rise in pulse rate and temperature. Sometimes a colic due to an impaction will manifest itself with a quiet and dull animal, lying down frequently, or just standing still with his hindquarters stretched out behind him.

When you first notice any of these signs, taking the horse out for a twenty-minute hand walk and a short graze will sometimes help. If the symptoms subside, let the horse rest in a well-bedded stall for an hour but do not leave him unattended as he may roll, causing further injury. After this time, if all symptoms have subsided offer him a small bran mash. However, if having hand walked him you see no improvement, call your vet immediately. After a bout of colic the horse should be started back into work gently and gradually, as it will often leave him weak and tired.

Of course, it is preferable to prevent the possibilities of colic occurring, and this can be achieved by adhering to the ages-old feeding rules and following a steady programme. Always feed a bran mash before a day off, and cut the feed in half on a rest day. All other changes in the feeding routine should be gradual.

Tieing-up

Another name for this is azoturia, or 'Monday morning disease'. The horse begins to show signs of stiffness behind, which increase until he is unable to move without great pain. With horses that are on a high-protein diet it can happen on the day after a rest day – hence 'Monday morning disease'. The muscles will feel hard to the touch, the horse may begin to sweat, and his temperature may even rise. He may find it difficult to urinate, and if he does urinate it will be darker than normal and may smell like violets.

During a Three-Day Event, tieing-up is classically seen immediately after the Steeplechase or in the Box. You must be very careful if your horse is scheduled to do his dressage on a Thursday and therefore has a free day before the Cross-Country.

When you suspect that your horse is tieing-up, stop work immediately, dismount, loosen his girth and cover his loins with your jacket or whatever is available. Walk him home slowly. If you are some distance away from base, ask for help so that he can be transported back to the stable. (Too much walking can lead to severe muscle damage.) Then call the vet. Back at the stable, keep the horse warm and comfortable. Massage the affected muscles and apply hot packs. Allow him to drink a little, as this will encourage him to stale, which will bring some relief until the vet arrives to administer muscle relaxants and other helpful medication.

A horse that has tied-up once is likely to have it happen again, so to prevent a recurrence, great attention must be paid to exercise and diet. If you think that there may be an imbalance, ask the vet to take an extra blood count. Avoid high-protein, heating food. Always reduce feed considerably on rest days; give a boiled feed or mash.

Make sure that the horse is turned out or taken for a hand walk. He should never be left in his stall all day. All exercise should begin very gradually, and an hour's walking before serious work should be part of your daily routine. After work it is also important to make sure that the horse is completely cooled down, by walking him; in the same way, a human athlete prevents muscle-cramps by doing loosening-up and cooling-down exercises before and after running a long distance. In very cold weather a quarter sheet should be used on a clipped horse to prevent his muscles from tightening. The vet will give you special vitamin and selenium additives to mix with his daily feed. A tried and trusted preventive measure is to add each day four ounces of sodium bicarbonate to the susceptible horse's water or feed bucket.

The Legs

We cannot emphasise too much the importance of each horse's individuality and of the essential care and attention that should be tailor-made for his own particular needs. All this is learned over a long period of time. Each day you should add a new clue to your jigsaw-like picture of your horses, until you have such , a knowledge and comprehensive history of each that the smallest change is immediately

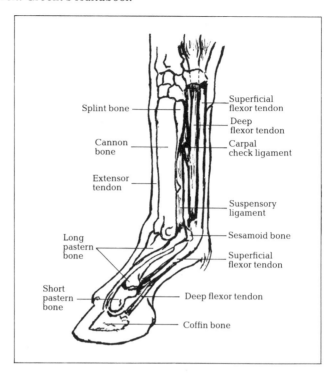

Splint bone

Cannon
bone

Extensor
tendon

Long
pastern
bone

Short
pastern
bone

Superficial
flexor tendon

Deep
flexor tendon

Carpal
check ligament

Suspensory
ligament

Sesamoid bone

Superficial
flexor tendon

Deep flexor tendon

Coffin bone

noticeable. By making leg-checking a part of your daily routine you will be able to pinpoint early-warning signals of stress, strain or trauma, and thus prevent further damage.

Basically, if heat, swelling and tenderness occur suddenly on a normal, sound leg this probably indicates acute injury, such as a bruise or a strain. Once you have discovered the cause you can decide with your rider and/or vet how you are going to treat it. One method is rest and a reduction in food, together with cold-temperature treatment – such as cold hosing for twenty minutes three or four times a day; standing the horse in a stream; applying a cold water bandage, cold poultices or ice-packs to the affected area; or the use of whirlpool boots. The reason that we cold-hose or use some other form of cold treatment immediately is to reduce further swelling and heat. (It is important to note that when hosing the legs you should always grease the heels and dry them thoroughly.) In the case of a bruise or knock, in which blood vessels are damaged and haemorrhaging, cold treatment will cause the dilated blood vessels to contract, and will thus limit the bruising. Hot treatments, such as hot compresses, hot poultices, sweats, and blisters, are, on the other hand, useful for *chronic* injuries or for the reduction of old scar tissue or thickenings that are left after an injury has healed and cooled out. Hot treatment increases circulation, so if applied to an injury within the first 36 hours it will cause excess haemorrhaging, thus increasing the damage and encouraging the bruising.

You may find that your horse is regularly 'stocked-up'. This is when two or all four legs are thicker from the hock or knee down to the foot. It is usually due either to poor circulation, lack of exercise, or too rich a diet. Decide which of the three could be the cause, and try to eliminate it. Dry, warm, stable bandages will increase circulation, thus helping to reduce the thickening.

If you discover an injury that has broken the skin, the cut or puncture must be cleaned hygienically. Check carefully that there are no foreign bodies still in the wound. Clip the hair around the area, apply an antiseptic ointment, and bandage. Any open wound should heal from the inside outwards, and you must clean and check it daily to prevent infection. In the case of a deep puncture or a wound needing stitches, always call the vet. If there is an infection, your vet may want to administer antibiotic injections.

One point of which you should be extremely wary is in the case of hot, tender and swollen joints or legs caused by neglected boot rubs, cracked heels, or mud fever. The obvious remedy, taking into account the heat and tenderness, would be cold-hosing. DON'T! Contact with water or poultice could increase the problem by causing even more infection. Treat the wound accordingly, and dry-wrap if necessary. If there is already quite an infection, which will show up in the horse's temperature, the vet may administer antibiotic injections.

Should you find heat in just one foot, with the pulse in the heel stronger than the pulse in the corresponding foot, you have discovered one of a number of foot problems. Jog the horse to see if he is sound. Probably he is not. Think of the possible causes. Could it be a stone bruise? Has he just been shod? If so, has he been 'pricked' or shod too tightly? Could he have an abscess? Usually either the blacksmith or the vet will help you with this problem. The treatment will most probably be removal of the shoe; rest; and either cold or hot tubbing (with Epsom salts) followed by a poultice. If the foot does not get better in a few days, there possibly could be bone-changes taking place, and your vet may think that X-rays are necessary.

Sore Backs and Muscles

Because of the number of hours spent by a rider on the horse's back in training – especially with older animals – their backs can become sore, as can their 'top line' muscles. Other causes of soreness are ill-fitting tack, rollers put on too tight with insufficient padding underneath, bad riding, or a fall on the cross-country.

If there are abrasions or rubs in the saddle area, treat the wounds and relieve the pressure spots by staying off the horse's back until the sore places have healed. To prevent a recurrence of the injuries, correct any saddle defects and place a piece of thick foam under the roller.

Other methods of relieving sore, tired muscles are:

Massaging with a diluted liniment, using the palm and heel of your hand, treating all the muscles on the horse's neck, shoulders and hindquarters, then covering them with a woollen cooler. (*Note* Whenever you use a liniment, read the instructions carefully. Some can cause blistering from over-use or from inadequate dilution.)

Heat lamps (to be used only under correct supervision).

Muscle stimulators, which by loosening up the muscles cause them to contract and relax, thus increasing the circulation. A stimulator can also help with specific muscle injuries. But you should not use it without consulting your vet.

If turnout areas are not available, or when turnout is not advisable in the case of a particular injury, a hand walk in the afternoon helps to prevent the muscles from stiffening up.

Vital Signs

Every horse is an individual, and once you leave 'resting' rates, normal figures can vary widely both in terms of the individual horse and also with that same horse in different environments, where heat, humidity, noise, etc, will all change. It is therefore essential to be familiar with each horse's particular characteristics, and this is where a sixth sense is important.

The normal 'resting' rates are:

Temperature: 100.5°F or 39.5°C.

Pulse: 35 to 40 beats per minute

Respiration: 10 to 12 breaths per minute

At the end of the Cross-Country the temperature can go up by four or five degrees, especially in hot weather; the pulse rate will be at least 100 – and usually nearer 200; respiration can be up to 100.

If the horse is fit, these figures should return pretty well to normal after half an hour. On the other hand, the figures can be different at this stage if the horse is in a strange environment and is not acclimatised, but can still be 'normal' for that horse at that time. Hence the importance of your sixth sense.

Glossary

Many of the following words, rather than being technical terms, are just words and phrases that are peculiar to either North America or Great Britain. Because this book has been written for both sides of the Atlantic, it contains both American and British expressions. This glossary has, therefore, been compiled to help clear up any misunderstandings.

Adhesion Fibrous knot of scar tissue that has formed between the layers of muscle fibre. It appears when the muscle has been bruised or inflamed and has been allowed to heal slowly on its own. The adhesion can be felt as a hard lump in the muscle mass and, if deep-seated, can cause stiffness.

Anti-sweat sheet Thin net-like sheet or rug, used to cover a sweating horse.

Automatic water bowl/drinker Mechanism that allows the horse to refill his water bowl every time he takes a drink. It ensures that the horse always has water, thus cutting down on labour.

Autumn British term meaning Fall.

Bandage British term for a leg wrap.

Banks (walls) The thick edges of a bed in a stable, giving it somewhat the appearance of a nest. The banks prevent horses from getting cast and help to eliminate draughts.

Barn American version of a stable or yard. In Britain, a barn is a building used mainly for storing hay and straw.

Bell boot American term for an over-reach boot. As its name implies, it is bell-shaped and protects the heel from an over-reach. It is a rubber, cuff-like boot that is pulled over the horse's foot and is worn around the pastern.

Billet Small metal hook-like fastening at the end of the reins and cheek pieces that secures the piece of leather that loops around the bit.

Blanket American term meaning a rug. In Britain, a blanket is a rectangular piece of warm material that fits under the shaped rug.

Borium American term for the extra dots of melted metal that the blacksmith puts on the toes and heels of shoes to give more traction, particularly on ice and snow. In Britain it is often called solder. It can be used to increase the life of a shoe.

Box (loose) British term meaning a stall, the enclosed indoor area in which a horse is stabled.

Box (the) The area at a Three-Day Event where the ten-minute compulsory halt is held between the end of Phase C and the beginning of Phase D. It is usually a roped or fenced-off area for the grooms, horses, riders, and coaches only.

Braid American term to describe a plait.

Bridle numbers Small numbers that are attached to the side of the bridle where the browband meets the headpiece. Normally used in the Dressage and Show Jumping phases.

Broken-out Term to describe the situation when the horse has been put away in his stable after work and, having dried off, starts to sweat again. Usually indicates that the horse is either unwell or was not sufficiently cooled out in the first place.

Bruised sole Though the sole, the flat underside of the foot, has little feeling of its own on the surface, it can bruise just like the bottom of your own foot, especially if it is constantly allowed to come in contact with rocky ground. A bruised sole can cause lameness and can be seen on the sole as a dark or red mark. It is very sensitive to pressure.

'Bute' Shortened slang version of the trade name, Butazolodine, which is given to the anti-inflammatory and pain-killing drug used in the treatment of various injuries and illnesses in the horse. It is now illegal at most international competitions, except in very small doses.

Cannon bone The main bone that runs from the horse's knee (and hock) down to the fetlock (ankle).

Caravan British term meaning a camper.

Chef d'Equipe Team manager at an international competition.

Clenches The tops of the horse-shoe nails that come through the wall of the foot and are hammered down flush with the wall. When a clench 'rises' it means that it has loosened, is protruding through the hoof and is no longer smoothly flush with the outer wall of the foot.

Clip To remove all or part of a horse's coat with a pair of electric clippers.

Coach American term meaning a trainer.

Colic drench A liquid medicine that is administered to the horse orally, usually with a plastic bottle or a syringe.

Cooled out Expression used when a horse that has been hot and blowing has been gradually walked in hand, so that he recovers his breath, and his pulse and temperature return to normal.

Cooler A large rectangular blanket made of very light-weight wool and used extensively in America. Excellent for throwing over a hot, sweaty horse, as it allows plenty of air to circulate whilst ensuring that the horse does not catch a chill. It reaches from the horse's ears right down to the tail, and to the knees and hocks.

Cross ties A way of tying the horse in a stable aisle or horse box by means of two lead lines. Instead of the horse being tied by one line, he is secured by two, one from either side of his headcollar. They are supposed to keep him straighter but can cause a horse to hurt himself if he pulls back, as it is not easy to break loose from them. Seen almost everywhere in the USA, but seldom in Britain.

Curb Fibrous swelling of the ligament that runs down the back of the hind leg from the point of the hock. It is formed when the ligament becomes strained and then swollen. Once the heat and pain have subsided, a hard protruding lump will form just below the point of the hock. It is a sign of weak or over-worked hocks.

Drop fence Any fence found on the cross-country course where the landing is lower than the take-off. The bigger the drop, the more concussion the horse's front legs and feet will have to withstand.

Dustbin   British term meaning a trash can.

Easyboot   A plastic boot that acts as a temporary replacement shoe. It fits over the entire foot and protects the hoof from breaking and the sole from becoming bruised.

Electrolytes   A powdered supplement, obtainable from your vet or tack shop. May be added to the horse's feed or water and replaces salts and essential minerals that the horse may have lost through profuse sweating. The horse cannot store these salts, so it is a waste to feed them in colder conditions, or when the horse is not working. They are, however, necessary for working horses in hotter places, as they help to maintain correct body fluid retention.

Fast work   Any piece of work your horse does that involves galloping and that is aimed at increasing body and wind fitness.

Flake (of hay)   A section of hay, weighing approximately five to seven pounds. Each bale of hay is divided into approximately ten sections or 'flakes'.

Flaked maize   British feedstuff, resembling cornflakes in appearance. High in protein but may be too sharp in texture for horses with sore mouths.

Flashlight   American term meaning a torch.

Floating (of teeth)   American version of rasping, which is when the dentist or vet files down the sharp edges of a horse's molars.

Gamgee   Protective wrap used extensively under bandages in Britain. Consists of soft protective padding within outside layers of gauze.

Hack   British term meaning a trail ride. Usually a long slow ride out for the horse, lasting anywhere between half an hour to two hours. The main reasons for hacking are to exercise the horse, to relax him, build up muscle and toughen up ligaments and tendons. Should be carried out on a long rein and may include short, fun trots and canters.

Halter   American term meaning a headcollar. Not to be confused with a rope halter.

Hard grain   Any grain that is hard and fairly high in protein, i.e. oats, barley, maize, and even some of the manufactured mixes.

Headcollar   See Halter.

Hock boot   Protective boot normally made of felt and re-inforced with leather. Worn over a horse's hocks to protect him from injury while travelling.

Horse box   British term meaning a van, a vehicle in which horses are transported.

'In front'   Refers to anything to do with the horse's front legs, i.e. put boots on in front.

'Interfering'   American term meaning brushing. Refers to the horse banging one leg or foot, or part of it, against the opposite leg or foot, normally causing an injury. Boots can be used for protection, and sometimes shoeing can correct this fault.

Jogging Also known as trotting in hand. This is when a person, positioned on the horse's near (left) side, trots the horse up and down, usually for the vet or owner, to determine soundness.

Joint (of fetlock) American version of fetlock joint, meaning the joint between the cannon bone and pastern. Also known as an 'ankle' in the USA.

Knee pads Similar to the hock boot in construction but used to protect the knees when travelling. They are also used to a great extent in Britain when riding on the roads, to protect the knees should the horse slip and fall.

Lead shank American version of lead rope. Also called a lead line.

Leg brace Topical astringent applied to the legs to tighten and cool them. Often used after work.

Let down Refers to the horse being gradually taken out of work and rested. Let down, roughed off, turned away, are all phrases meaning to rest the horse and to turn him out into the field for a holiday.

Ligaments Tough bands of tissue that join bones to bones. Found extensively in the joint areas.

Milk teeth Just as humans have milk teeth, so do horses. They lose them all by the time they are six years old. Though the incisors are then permanent, the molars grow continually, to keep up with the wearing process.

Minimum weight In international senior competitions, and in some national events, horses are required to carry a minimum weight to ensure that everyone has the same handicap. This weight is normally 165 lbs – or 11 st. 11 lbs., or 75 kgs.

Muzzle Bucket-shaped guard made of leather, wire-mesh or plastic, that fits over the lower half of the horse's head, i.e. his mouth and nostrils. It has air holes to enable easy breathing and to allow the horse to drink, but prevents him from eating his bedding, bandages, or clothing. It may be attached to a headcollar or slipped over the ears like a halter.

Neutral zone (safe area) Pre-designated area on a Three-Day Event course, where a rider may have legal assistance without the fear of being eliminated. These areas can be found at the end of the Steeplechase phase (B) and in the ten-minute Box between Phases C and D.

New Zealand rug A canvas waterproof rug that was originally designed in New Zealand, for use on horses living out in the open. It is toughly constructed and is often wool-lined. Sometimes referred to as a 'turn-out' rug.

Omnibus schedule Both the British and the American organisations dealing with Horse Trials publish a booklet bi-annually that lists and describes the registered competitions held throughout the year. This enables the rider to see what Events are available and gives him all the information he needs to make his entries.

Over girth   The girth that goes over the saddle and secures with a buckle under the horse's stomach. It is usually made of canvas and is a safety precaution in case the girth attached to the saddle should break.

Over-reach   An injury to the back of the pastern or bulbs of the heel, due to the toe of the hind foot coming forward and catching the front foot. It usually happens during galloping and jumping, when the front feet do not move soon enough out of the way of the hind feet.

Pad   Piece of leather or plastic that goes against the sole under the shoe to protect the foot from bruising. Used extensively on terrain that is rocky.

Parasite   An organism or creature that lives on or inside an animal. Flies, ticks and fleas are external parasites; worms are internal. Horses suffer from internal parasites mainly because of poor management of land, where horses are grazed on infested pasture.

Pellets   American term for nuts or cubes.

Poultice   A mud-like paste that can be used to soothe or draw out infection. Often used to relieve hot, tired legs after competitions. Used hot, a poultice will increase circulation.

Pricked   The term used when a shoeing nail is driven up into the sensitive part of the foot. The nail should stay within the confines of the insensitive wall of the foot but, occasionally, the blacksmith will misjudge its thickness and the nail will 'prick' the inside of the foot. If this is not remedied by removal of the shoe and thorough cleaning of the wound, the area will fester and the horse will become lame.

Quartering   An old-fashioned term meaning to brush the horse off quickly, usually first thing in the morning. It is called quartering because it is done while the rugs are still on the horse; the front of the rug is folded back while the front of the horse is being brushed and then the back of the rug is folded forward for the quarters to be done.

Rug   British term for a blanket.

Saddle pad   American term for a numnah.

Saran wrap   American term for cling film.

Season   In Britain there are two seasons every year in the Eventing calendar – Spring, which is usually March to June, and Autumn, which is August to October. In the USA, because of the vast area and great climatic differences, the season extends from February to December.

Spavin (bone)   Hard bony lump that appears on the front inside and lower edge of the hock. It can be the result of over-strain or of a direct blow.

'Spreading'   Used to describe a horse shoe that has spread away from the foot. Usually it will show by sticking out at the side. If the shoe spreads on the inside, it may catch and injure the opposite leg.

Stadium jumping   American term for Show Jumping. Strictly speaking, in Combined Training the correct name for this test is Jumping.

Stall   American term for a loose box, the enclosed area in which a horse is stabled. In Britain, stall describes the old-fashioned stabling area, where a horse was tied up, facing the manger.

Stall guard   Either a webbing or a plastic guard that goes across the doorway of a stall. It allows the horse to look out and can be used on temporary stalls that have no doors. Used extensively in the USA.

Starting times   At Combined Training competitions, each competitor is given the exact starting times for the Dressage and Cross-Country tests. In the case of Two-Day and Three-Day Events, exact times are also given for all four phases of the Speed and Endurance Test. This keeps everything running smoothly and efficiently.

String vest   See Anti-sweat sheet.

Studs   Metal cleats that are screwed into the heels of the shoe to give more grip. Various types and sizes are used according to the condition of the ground.

Surcingle   A canvas, webbing, or leather strap that secures a rug to a horse. In Britain, a padded roller is more commonly used, as it helps to prevent pressure on the spine.

Sweat   A method of reducing old or chronic fillings or thicknesses by encouraging a 'drawing' or 'sweating' effect. This is done by plastering the area with a grease-based antiseptic cream, then covering it with a plastic 'wrap', followed by Gamgee and a bandage. It increases circulation and can be used to reduce fibrous lumps. Used extensively in the USA.

Tendons   Tough cords of dense fibrous tissue that connect muscle to other parts. They are the force behind the power of the muscles.

Thrush   A disorder in the feet, recognised by the bad smell and black, creamy, stinking discharge found in the cleft of the frog. It is a bacterial or fungal infection, caused by forcing the horse to stand continually on a filthy bed. Usually remedied with plenty of cleansing and the use of antiseptic powders.

Topical   Word found on many veterinary and equine products, such as fly sprays, ointments and blisters. It is an indication of how they are to be used and means that the substance must only be applied to the outer skin and must not be taken internally (swallowed). A 'topical' injury refers to a surface wound.

Trace minerals   Essential minerals that horses normally obtain from the ground and from plants when they are living in a natural state out in the fields. They can be given through electrolytes.

Troughs   Metal or concrete containers for water, commonly seen in Britain. They are about eight feet long and are placed in most fields so that the horse always has a supply of water.

Truck   American vehicle, often used to tow a trailer.

Tubbing   Refers to the practice of soaking a horse's foot in a bucket of warm water, to which salt has been added to act as a disinfectant. It is a soothing method of drawing out bruising or infection.

Van   American version of a horse box, used for the transportation of horses.

Weight cloth   Cloth or leather pad that has pockets for the lead bars that some riders must carry, in order to make the minimum weight. The lead should be distributed equally between the pockets.

Windgalls   Enlargements of the fluid sac (bursa) located immediately above the fetlocks (ankles). They are a sign of strain or concussion but are not considered an unsoundness and are usually not painful.

Wolf teeth   Little teeth that are the remnants of the premolars of the prehistoric horse. They sometimes remain dormant but more often break through the gums of a young horse. They are situated immediately in front of the molars and are usually removed as they can interfere with the action of the bit.

Worm count   A manure sample, examined by a vet under a microscope, in order to count the worm infestation. All horses play host to some worms but the vet will be able to tell you if your horse is overly infected and needs worming.

Worming   The administration of a worm-killing medicine that can be given every six to eight weeks to rid the horse of internal parasites. There are different types of medicine to treat the various species of worms.

Wrap   See Bandage.

Yard   British version of the American barn, which describes the whole stable area.

The culmination of a successful grooming career can lead to exciting stable management projects. Here the authors met the challenge as stable managers of the 1984 Los Angeles Olympic Games.

171

Index

Page numbers in **bold** refer to illustrations